PENGUIN PASSNOTES

English Language

Jill Talbot was educated at Hove County School and Leeds Training College. She has recently retired from the teaching profession. For twenty years she taught English and has had wide experience of preparing students for the G.C.E. O-level Language and Literature examinations. She now lives in Brighton where she works as a writer, mainly in the educational field. She has also written the study guide to *Great Expectations* in the Passnotes series.

PENGUIN PASSNOTES

English Language

JILL TALBOT

ADVISORY EDITOR: STEPHEN COOTE, M.A., PH.D.

PENGUIN BOOKS

Penguin Books Ltd, Harmondsworth, Middlesex, England
Viking Penguin Inc., 40 West 23rd Street, New York, New York 10010, U.S.A.
Penguin Books Australia Ltd, Ringwood, Victoria, Australia
Penguin Books Canada Limited, 2801 John Street, Markham, Ontario, Canada L3R 1B4
Penguin Books (N.Z.) Ltd, 182–190 Wairau Road, Auckland 10, New Zealand

First published 1984
Reprinted 1984, 1985, 1986

Filmset in Monophoto Ehrhardt by
Northumberland Press Ltd, Gateshead
Made and printed in Great Britain by
Richard Clay (The Chaucer Press) Ltd, Bungay, Suffolk

*The publishers are grateful to the following Examination Boards for
permission to reproduce questions from examination papers used in
individual titles in the Passnotes series:*

*Associated Examining Board, University of Cambridge Local
Examinations Syndicate, Joint Matriculation Board, University of
London School Examinations Department, Oxford and Cambridge Schools
Examination Board, University of Oxford Delegacy of Local
Examinations.*

*The Examination Boards accept no responsibility whatsoever for the
accuracy or method of working in any suggested answers given as models.*

Contents

4 COMPOSITION 135

1 Basic Skills

READING

English language is part of your life and should be as natural to you as waking and sleeping. What you have to do for the examination is sharpen your skills. Take a critical look at your achievements so far: assess your strengths and weaknesses, plan your study time, and work through these pages until you have stretched your inborn ability to its limit and your command of the language has become second nature.

Every year the examiners give us valuable guides to better marks. They issue reports on the previous year's examinations, and explain why they awarded or deducted marks and what they thought about the candidates' work. They criticize the scripts on two levels: they give their general impression of the examination as a whole, and back up their comments with detailed summaries of their observations in each section. In a nutshell, they say: 'Never be satisfied with less than your best.'

I shall refer to their comments and advice from time to time so that you know what pitfalls to avoid. Our starting-point is a remark which contains a vital clue to your success: 'There seem to be increasing numbers of words spelt as they are heard, indicating perhaps that children are reading less, and watching and listening more . . .'

Although spelling is important and will be discussed later (see pp. 24–33), there is a hint in those words even more important. The words 'children are reading less' contain a wealth of implied advice: if you do not read, you put yourself at a serious disadvantage. You will lack not only the basic spelling skills, but also ideas; the capacity to think, feel and understand; the ability to express yourself fluently; and, of course, you will miss out on a great deal of pleasure.

Candidates who read regularly rarely fail the English Language examination, for they learn the writer's craft from experts, almost without realizing it.

Paragraph Study

Until your sentences flow smoothly and your vocabulary, spelling and punctuation improve, concentrate your mind on the written word.

Take any paragraph at random – preferably from a well-known modern book, but certainly not from a magazine or newspaper. Read it and pay attention to the writer's choice of words and phrases. Look up the meanings of those you are unable to define. If you are uncertain about any, make a point of asking someone to help you.

In your paragraph study, look at the sentences and ask yourself these questions:

1. Do they vary in length?
2. Do they make complete sense?
3. How do they begin and end?
4. Why have the various punctuation marks been used?
5. How many sentences make the paragraph?
6. Which is the key sentence – or topic sentence?
7. How are the other sentences related to it?
8. Read the paragraph aloud and listen to the sound of the words.

WORKED EXAMPLE: Take the paragraph that begins the comprehension test on p. 90. Apply the concentration exercise just suggested, and compare your findings with mine.

When we pay attention to the words we notice especially:

February ... snow-storm ... smothered ... drifts ... bleak ... burying ... by the dozen ... huddled ... blinded by the blizzard ... abandoned ... blocked ... raged ... blustered ... subsided ... sullen ... transfigured

These words build up a picture of the violence of the storm, and the desolation of the scene. The word 'smothered' is exceptionally well chosen, anticipating death and destruction. Which did you write down? Probably 'blustered', which means 'stormed noisily', and 'transfigured', which means 'changed in appearance'.

Now ask yourself the basic questions above. Answers:

1. Yes, the sentences do vary in length.
2. Each one makes complete sense.
3. Every sentence begins with a capital letter and ends with a full stop. (A sentence can also end with a question mark or an exclamation mark.)
4. (i) To indicate a short pause a comma precedes the phrase 'burying by the dozen the huddled sheep'. Watch out for more phrases like this. They often introduce a sentence and begin with a word ending in '-ing'. This one is related to the word 'drifts'.

    (ii) In the fourth sentence, another phrase is separated from the main sentence by commas. Two are needed this time because the phrase is in the middle of the sentence. It relates to 'van'.

    (iii) Later in the same sentence, a further comma is required before the final phrase.

    All these commas indicate a short pause to the reader.

    (iv) Look very carefully at the last sentence. Nine candidates out of ten would have wrongly used a comma here. A comma will not do because a longer pause is needed. In the extract two main ideas – complete in themselves – have been separated by a semicolon so that the reader pauses to consider the content of the first part of the sentence before going on to the detail contained in the second part. As the two ideas are connected, a semicolon is an accurate and skilful mark to use (see p. 15). Other correct ways of presenting those two main ideas would be: 'By Friday its fury had subsided. A sullen sun gleamed from the ashen sky on to a transfigured landscape.' Or: 'By Friday its fury had subsided, and a sullen sun gleamed from the ashen sky on to a transfigured landscape.' However, a semicolon is more effective here.

    (v) Notice 'its' in 'its fury' – just simply '*its*' and nothing else (see pp. 18–19, 27 and 34).
5. Six sentences form the paragraph.
6. The key sentence is the first one.
7. The other five sentences add detail about the blizzard.

8. You must have heard the effectiveness of 'blinded by the blizzard', 'sullen sun' and the repetition of the soft sounds throughout the paragraph.

THE RULES OF WRITTEN ENGLISH

These comments come from a recent examiners' report:

The most obvious faults of punctuation, grammar, syntax [the order of words in a sentence] and spelling were as prevalent as ever, and the Chief Examiners' policy in assessing such faults remained the same: whenever the error, of whatever kind, confused or misled the reader, or seriously impeded the expression of the candidate's thoughts, then a significantly adverse adjustment was made in recording the candidate's ability.*

In other words, candidates who break the rules of written English lose several marks, and in many cases fail the examination.

In this section we shall revise the skills mentioned one at a time.

Punctuation

All punctuation is important, but the most common errors are: (a) using a comma where a stronger full stop is essential, and (b) not knowing how to use apostrophes properly.

The best way to put punctuation errors behind you is to read good writing carefully – just as we were doing in the worked example about the blizzard – until you can punctuate automatically.

Look again at the extract on p. 90. In poor written work it would not be unusual to read commas where full stops are printed. Read as far as 'sheep' and explain why it would be incorrect to use commas where the author has used full stops. Notice how a comma does not allow the sense of the words to come across, since it indicates only a slight pause and does not announce the end of a sentence; a longer pause is necessary after 'came' and 'Riding' to indicate that a statement has been made and each sentence is finished.

* Associated Examining Board: Reports of Examiners, June Examination 1980.

FULL STOP OR EQUIVALENT (a long pause):

———. A statement made followed by a full stop.

———? A question asked followed by a question mark. Only one should be used at a time.

———! An exclamation, order or command followed by an exclamation mark. Only one should be used at a time.

... Three full stops mean that words have been left out.

COMMA (a short pause): Commas divide words or groups of words from the rest of the sentence to make the writer's words clear to the reader. Cover up the explanations of the following examples and see if you understand why the commas have been used.

The examples of punctuation quoted below are taken from the passage set for Summary and Directed Writing, June 1981 (see p. 45) and the blizzard passage on p. 90.

	EXAMPLES	EXPLANATION
(i)	'rain, wind, snow, fog or ice ...'	Commas separate two or more words in a list.
(ii)	'... a house in London, another in the country, and a third on the French Riviera ...'	Commas separate two or more groups of words.
(iii)	'Tommy Lawton, the football hero of the forties, spent his later years in poverty ...' ('Tommy Lawton' *and* 'the football hero of the forties' *are the same person.*)	Used in pairs, commas separate words or groups of words to make the sense clearer.
(iv)	'Perhaps, after all, it is better to remain a keen amateur.' ('after all' *is an aside remark.*)	Used in a pair here.
(v)	'Madam, you are trespassing ...' or 'Do you know, Madam, you are trespassing?' (*Quotation altered slightly for the sake of an example.*)	Commas enclose the name of a person or group being spoken to.

	EXAMPLES	EXPLANATION
(vi)	'The Council Library van, blinded by the blizzard, was abandoned in a blocked ditch ...' ('blinded by the blizzard' *describes the van's windows*.)	If you remove the words enclosed in commas, the sentence still makes sense. See also (iii), (iv) and (v).
(vii)	'Drifts blew across the bleak stretches of Cold Harbour Colony, burying by the dozen the huddled sheep.'	Words that need to be marked off from the rest are not always inside the sentence. They often appear at the end.
(viii)	'A wild wind blew the seagulls about the esplanade, wheeling and shrieking.'	See (vii).
(ix)	'Scuttering and slithering over the rutted snow, she passed through three open gateways ...'	They appear at the beginning, too.
(x)	'Scuttering and slithering over the rutted snow, she passed through three open gateways, and found herself right on the edge of the cliff, where, sure enough, according to plan, she saw the track of the "hares" leading down a slope where the earth had fallen on to the snow-covered shore.'	Note again the comma after the 'ing' phrase: 'sure enough' and 'according to plan' could be removed without altering the sense of the sentence.

Read the complete sentence above (x), and you will automatically make pauses where the commas are printed. They separate the groups of words to make the sense clearer.

N.B. A comma is used only when the sense demands it. *When in doubt leave out.*

The worst thing you can do is to use a comma instead of a full stop. In the examples printed in this section, you will find examples to help you understand how and when to use a comma, or a pair of commas. Please note that it is *never* used to separate one complete statement from another.

Commas are also used with 'link words':

	EXAMPLES	EXPLANATION
(i)	'It is always attractive to do something interesting and to do it as well as possible, but serious injury or an unaccountable loss of form quickly halts the progress of many a young sportsman.' ('But' *is the link word*.)	Commas are used with 'link words' when sentences are joined together.
(ii)	'If any damage has been done, we will of course pay compensation.' ('If' *is the link word*.) You would not be wrong to put commas before and after 'of course' in the above example.	The order of this sentence could have been: 'We will of course pay compensation, if any damage has been done.' The link word is now in the middle, but the sense is the same.

The comma is used before the link word only when the sense demands it, or an obvious pause requires it. *When in doubt leave out.*

Here are some useful link words that you can use after a comma:

after	before	since
although	but	unless
and	for	until
as	if	when
because	lest	while

N.B. Remember that the link words can also begin the sentence: see (ii) above.

Warning: The following are *not* link words or link phrases and *cannot* be used after a comma to join sentences together:

accordingly	in this way	then
for instance	thus	therefore
however	on the other hand	nevertheless
in fact	so	yet

If you want to connect sentences with any of the above use a *semi-colon* first (see p. 15).

INVERTED COMMAS OR QUOTATION MARKS: Look out for inverted commas. As well as being used to enclose the words that people speak, inverted commas are used for other purposes in handwritten pieces. These marks may be "double" or 'single' – both are correct and usage will vary from board to board. Be *consistent* when you use them.

Use inverted commas or quotation marks for *titles* of books, plays, poems, radio and television programmes; *names* of newspapers, magazines, ships; *quotations*: single words taken from a passage and longer quotations; and for *words that should not be taken literally.* (N.B. When you are reading you may see *titles* of books, etc. and *names* of newspapers and ships printed in italic without quotation marks. This is also correct, but for the purposes of your written examination, it is clearer to use inverted commas.)

Here is an indication of how to punctuate direct speech (the words people actually say):

	EXAMPLES	EXPLANATION
(i)	She said proudly, 'I will take all responsibility.'	First word inside inverted commas always has a capital letter. Note full stop inside inverted commas.
(ii)	'I will take all responsibility,' she said proudly.	Note comma inside inverted commas. Note small letter 's'.
(iii)	'I will,' she said proudly, 'take all responsibility.'	Note comma inside inverted commas. Note small letter 's'; note small letter 't'; and note full stop inside inverted commas.

Look carefully at the actual words spoken: 'I will take all responsibility.' The sentence begins with a capital letter and ends with a full stop. You will agree that this is normal and that is how it is punctuated in example (i).

But what has happened in example (ii)? The words spoken finish with a comma, because the sentence goes on to 'she said proudly'. As the full stop is due at the end of a *complete* sentence, it follows 'proudly'.

In the last example the spoken words have been interrupted by 'she said proudly', therefore 'take' is in the middle of the sentence and thus needs a small 't'. The full stop comes at the end of the *complete* sentence.

SEMICOLON: Do your utmost to learn how to use this. The semicolon is a useful punctuation mark and using it correctly impresses your readers – especially the examiners.

EXAMPLE	EXPLANATION
'Considerable profits are made out of selling sports gear which is a replica of that used by the professionals; newspapers sell more copies if their sports coverage is good, and substantial gains can be made out of the spectators' willingness to gamble on results.' (Connected by the idea of 'profits'.)	The semicolon separates two connected sentences. The reader is forced to pause.

When you want to use a semicolon check that you are separating ideas that could each easily be in one sentence. The ideas above are all right because they can become one sentence on the strength of the idea of profits. Related ideas can always be punctuated with semicolons. Check that the ideas on either side of the semicolon are complete in themselves.

THE APOSTROPHE 'S': The worst thing you can do with an apostrophe 's' is to use it without thinking. Once you have understood its basic function, you will always use this mark correctly. The apostrophe 's' is always a sign of ownership, and you must learn to recognize it. Once an apostrophe 's' has been attached to a word, that word owns something and its possession is the next word in the line. Look at these examples:

1. *Singular*:
    (i)   Sarah's feelings: the feelings belonged to Sarah.
    (ii) Miss Jameson's reactions: the reactions belonged to Miss Jameson.
    (iii) the afternoon's timetable: the timetable belonged to just one afternoon.

   Decide who (or what) is the owner and put an apostrophe at the end of that word followed by an 's'.

   Study these examples and decide whether what we have said so far makes sense: Who does the owning and what is owned?

   > woman's knitting
   > student's certificate
   > bicycle's tyres
   > tree's branches
   > ox's tail
   > robin's song

   Each time, in the examples above, there is only one owner: woman, student, bicycle, tree, ox and robin. The apostrophe 's' is the *sign of ownership* and must be attached to each owner to tell the reader that:

   > the woman owns the knitting
   > the student owns the certificate
   > the bicycle owns the tyres (or, put another way, the tyres belong to the bicycle)
   > the branches belong to the tree
   > the tail belongs to the ox
   > the song belongs to the robin

   In other words there is one owner each time.

2. *Plural*: It is a little more complicated when there are several owners.
    (i) If the plural word that denotes 'owners' does not end in an 's', you do exactly the same as we have been doing already. Many words form their plurals internally (e.g. tooth, *tee*th) or they stay the same whether singular or plural (sheep, sheep). It is these words that we are concentrating on at the moment. All you have to do is to punctuate them like this:

children's games
sportsmen's lives
sheep's fleeces

How many children, sportsmen, sheep? Definitely more than one each time. Because the words are plural (sheep must be plural in this case, because one sheep could not have more than one fleece) and do not end in 's', we show the ownership by giving them the "'s' sign in the simple way we used before.

(ii) More often than not, though, plurals are formed by adding 's' or 'es' to a word. What then? Study these:

students' certificates
bicycles' tyres
trees' branches
robins' songs

and decide whether you have solved the problems of using the apostrophe for possession. Were you able to recognize several owners each time in the last set of examples? They were students, bicycles, trees and robins and the apostrophe went after the 's' that made them plural.

It is not enough to understand the use of the apostrophe 's'. You must be bold as well. Put the mark clearly before the 's' or clearly after it; *never on top of it*. Such indecision is always counted wrong and marks are forfeited.

So far so good, but we cannot leave apostrophes without a brief reference to a few exceptions.

3. *Some difficult cases*: Sometimes an owner's name ends in 's'. What would you do then? There are no hard and fast rules and you may see different methods in your reading. The best tactic is to punctuate as before and write, for example, James's room, the princess's romance, the witness's evidence. There is no need to be afraid of expressions like these with three 's's' in a row when the words are easy to pronounce.

It is a different matter when the addition of 's' adds another syllable to a word already three or more syllables long. In such cases we would write 'the hippopotamus' feet', leaving out the 's' after the apostrophe even though the owner is singular.

One final point: if an owner ends with an 's' and the thing owned begins with an 's', the apostrophe works without its usual 's' to avoid too many 's's' in a row; otherwise there could sometimes be as many as four. Thus: 'the actress' signature'.

Your common sense should help you to decide about the exceptions. If they become tongue-twisters with too many 's's' or syllables, the apostrophe can be used on its own.

How would you re-phrase the following time expressions using an apostrophe?

a holiday of three weeks
a journey of eight hours
a wait of a week
the work of a month
the march of a day

The safest way would be to write:

three weeks' holiday
eight hours' journey
a week's wait
a month's work
a day's march

I say 'safest' because there has been some difference of opinion about what is correct and what is not. You will not be wrong if you use the apostrophe like this for all 'time expressions'.

Note: 'its' denotes belonging (e.g. 'Return the book to *its* place.') and *never* has an apostrophe. Learn the difference between 'its' (meaning ownership) and 'it's' (meaning 'it is' or 'it has' – see next entry).

THE APOSTROPHE INDICATING MISSING LETTERS (I've, they're, it's): The apostrophe has another use. Sometimes words are shortened in direct speech and these shortened words are called contractions. They are used in informal writing, too, but in formal writing – the kind you will use for Composition and most Summary and Comprehension tests – always write the words in full.

There is a growing tendency for contractions to appear in print in some formal writing, but examiners do not approve of them in

English Language papers. Naturally, you would use them if you wrote dialogue or an informal letter, but on the whole your best policy would be to write out the word in full.

CONTRACTION (*use for informal writing*)	IN FULL (*use for formal writing*)	APOSTROPHE STANDS FOR	NOTE ESPECIALLY
I've	I have	ha	
wouldn't	would not	o	
must've	must have	ha	'must *have*' (NOT 'must of')
isn't	is not	o	
can't	cannot	no	
they're	they are	a	Must *never* be confused with 'there' or 'their' (see p. 27). *Two* words: 'they are'.
it's	it is *or* it has	i *or* ha	'It is' *or* 'it has' and *nothing* else.
don't	do not	o	
would've	would have	ha	'would *have*' (NOT 'would of')

The apostrophe is always written in the space where the letter(s) is (are) missing.

THE REMAINING PUNCTUATION MARKS: Study these and then try the test on p. 21 when you understand them.

1. *Colon*: This is the 'something-will-follow' sign. It marks a pause long enough to take a breath and consider the words on either side of it.

It introduces: a list of words; a list of phrases; a list of longer groups of words; a quotation; or direct speech. It can also indicate (a) contrast or a direct opposite in a sentence, or (b) an explanation in the second part of the sentence of what has been said in the first part.

Beware of mixing your signs. A comma is more often used for introducing a quotation or direct speech. Decide which you prefer and keep to one *or* the other throughout your writing.

2. *Hyphen*: This mark is shorter than a dash. It has many uses, most of which need not concern you for your O-level examination.

A hyphen indicates:

(i) that a word has been split at the end of a line and the rest of the word is on the next line. Never begin a new line with only one letter following on from the last word in the line above. You must carry over at least two letters. However, you should beware of splitting words. It is better to squeeze up your writing at the end of a line, or leave a space and go on to the next line. If you *do* get caught, *split at syllables only*. If the word has a double letter, put your hyphen between them. Look out for examples in your reading. How many letters are there in hyphenated words? Notice that the hyphen is always placed at the *end* of the line, after the first part of the split word, *never* at the beginning of a line.

(ii) that two or more words have been joined together to make one word. What happens to the sense when you leave out the hyphen?

3. *Dash*: Use a single dash towards the end of a sentence. This indicates:

(i) an aside remark at the end of a sentence.

(ii) an abrupt interruption.

(iii) a word or part of a word has been left out.

(iv) the climax has been reached and what follows gathers up all that has been said.

(v) a witty ending to your sentence, or an anticlimax.

Do *not* fall into the trap of careless use. Use *sparingly*.

4. *Dashes*: Dashes used in pairs divide aside remarks and afterthoughts that contain information, illustration and explanation, from the main flow of the sentence. An aside remark or afterthought is called a

parenthesis. Say to yourself, 'I've started so I'll finish' when you begin a pair of dashes.

5. *Brackets*: Brackets are used for:
   (i) the same reasons as pairs of dashes. (Say 'I've started so I'll finish' again.)
   (ii) dividing longer passages from the mainstream of the writing.

All these remaining punctuation marks, listed 1–5 above, must be used with care. Over-use will reduce the quality of your work.

Before we leave this section on punctuation, take a close look at the following sentences:

1. The dream came true: Dickens lived at Gad's Hill for the last twelve years of his life ...

(adapted from: 'Charles Dickens: His Tragedy and Triumph', Edgar Johnson)
Explain the colon and the three dots.

2. The boys lashed the corn to the pew ends while the girls threaded cape gooseberries through the altar rails, and put a neat little row of plums – with a marrow at regular intervals – along the foot.

('Village Diary', Miss Read)
Explain the pair of dashes and the inverted commas around 'Village Diary'.

3. It all looked very formal and childlike – and none the less effective for that.
('Village Diary', Miss Read)

Explain the dash.

4 ... we returned ... to practise 'We plough the fields and scatter' ready for the great day. And so busy were Miss Jackson and I trying to wean our charges from singing: 'But it is fed and wor-hor-tered' that it was time to send them home before we knew where we were.
('Village Diary', Miss Read)

Explain the colon and the hyphens.

5 In the intervals of fitting her dress and of superintending a simply colossal spring cleaning of the farm (the first it had received for a hundred years) Flora kept a weather eye upon the affair of Mr Mybug and Rennet.
('Cold Comfort Farm', Stella Gibbons)

Explain the brackets.

6. And suddenly – the flash! It was over indeed: her long indecision and her bewilderment about how to deal with Aunt Ada Doom.

('Cold Comfort Farm', Stella Gibbons)

Explain the dash, the exclamation mark and the colon.

Now compare your answers with mine:

1. As the colon is the 'something-will-follow' sign, it leads the reader on to the detail about what the dream was and when it came true. The three dots mean that words have been left out.

2. The words 'with a marrow at regular intervals' are cut off from the rest of the sentence with dashes. This is a parenthesis. 'Village Diary' is enclosed in inverted commas as it is the title of a book.

3. The dash in this one indicates a change of thought. It is an aside remark at the end of the sentence.

4. This colon leads on to the words sung by the children which the writer is quoting. The hyphens make the made-up word clearer, and it is possible to imagine the children emphasizing the middle syllable 'hor'.

5. This is another parenthesis divided from the main sentence, this time by brackets. If you remove the words in brackets the sentence will still make sense. Is the same true if you remove the parenthesis in example 2?

6. The dash forces the reader to pause. This, in turn, emphasizes the exclamation. Imagine a full stop after 'flash' and read the four words again. Do you notice the difference? It seems like an anticlimax without the exclamation mark. The colon leads on to the explanation of what was over.

Do not be satisfied until you understand all these punctuation marks. When you take your examination, your papers will stand out from the rest if you can show that you have mastered this basic skill.

Year after year candidates who do not bother lose so many marks that the examiners have described the failure to punctuate accurately as 'the most expensive error of all'.

Vocabulary

Examiners are always looking for a wide vocabulary and for writing that has the power to convey feeling, excitement, compassion, surprise, impressions and insight. When we come to the Composition Section (see pp. 135–69), we shall discuss how to appeal to the reader's senses; meanwhile, do notice how writers move their readers to tears or laughter or fear or pity.

As they are the raw material for our craft, words must be carefully selected. We must choose as an artist chooses his colours or a gardener his seeds, with the power to see fine distinction and difference.

But words tarnish easily. When they are used incorrectly, or pronounced wrongly, or overworked, their brightness is dimmed and they become defiled. The examiners have criticized the use of these 'defiled' or 'tarnished' words and phrases. Avoid them unless you are sure that you know what you are doing. They are inferior raw material and those who use them unthinkingly produce shoddy goods.

Here is a list of some words and phrases that have been spoilt by overwork or incorrect usage and colloquial expressions that have no place in written English:

all-time greats	got
all-time low	gotten
almighty	got wise to
amazing	grind to a halt
best ever	grotty
bit	hassle
con	hopefully
cheers	however
chucked out	in this day and age
do your own thing	item
down the shops	large
fabulous	lot *and* lots of
fantastic	low profile
few and far between	materialize
get	meaningful
going on a bit	moan (meaning 'complain')
good (use only as defined in the	nice
dictionary)	no chance

no way
overall
off–putting
old boy
O.K.
or whatever
out of this world
pop off
really (instead of 'very')
tatty

that's it (as an ending)
thick (meaning 'dull')
thing
traumatic
uptight
up the park
vandalism
well (as the first word of a sentence)

This list has been compiled after studying several examiners' reports. Even if candidates use such expressions in spoken English, would you not expect them to make more effort in an examination? One report ended by quoting that in a particular answer about a relationship between two people, some candidates described it as 'dodgy' or 'a bit sticky' and said that one of them was 'kind of depressed' and 'going to pieces in a big way' but was advised to 'stick with it'. The other 'kept on moaning' at him, urging him to 'get himself sorted out'. But he 'couldn't care less'. The examiners regretted 'that candidates should have no language other than these weary clichés in which to express themselves'.

Many tarnished expressions are spoken on television, so when you switch on do be aware of the difference between formal and informal language. Always remember that written English must be correct English. There is no room for slang, clichés, colloquialism or vulgarity.

Spelling

Spelling matters. Make no mistake about that. Some unwise candidates adopt the attitude that they are poor spellers and there is nothing much they can do about it, except learn to live with their handicap. This is wrong. All they are saying, in effect, is that they are too lazy or too uninterested to bother.

Where do we begin? With a long, long list. All the words have been taken from candidates' work and examiners' reports. *They are the regular errors.* Let us put these right first. Your best plan of action would be to enlist the help of a friend and to work through the words together ticking all those that you know how to spell. Transfer the remainder to a small notebook, entering them in groups of ten. Add to this notebook every word that causes you a spelling problem whenever you come across it. Some words will be entered several times on different pages.

Learn the words systematically and when you realize you are using them correctly, without effort, tick them off. Learning to spell words one day, testing yourself the next and getting them all right, will probably encourage you; but do not be misled. You must allow time for the word patterns to penetrate your memory. Your memory will store a few words received regularly over a long period, but if you flood it too quickly the recently acquired knowledge will be washed away. Little and often is the best motto for success with spelling.

When you know the words on the long list, you can turn your attention to making sure you have the correct word patterns for words you hear. Most are not spelled as they are heard. Test yourself regularly.

If, after all your preparation and hard work, a particular spelling escapes you in the examination room, try to think of an alternative word.

WORDS THAT ARE OFTEN SPELLED INCORRECTLY

accept (receive or admit)	alcohol	autumn	bought (buy)
	almost	awful	Britain
accepted	already	awkward	broken
accidentally	also	bachelor	brought (bring)
accommodation	although	banister	business
achieve	always	beautiful	camouflage
achievement	amount	because	category
acquaintance	anxious	beginning	ceiling
across	appalled	behaviour	century
address	appalling	being	changeable
advantage	apparent	believe	character
advertisement	arctic	bicycle	chimneys
affair	argument	biscuit	choose
affect (influence)	associate	bodies	climbing
agreeable	author	bored	clothes

college
colour
comment
committee
competition
completely
conscience
conscious
corridor
countries
courageous
cries
damaged
deceive
decided
definitely
delicately
describe
desperate
deteriorated
develop
development
diary
difference
different
dining-room
disappeared
disappoint
disastrous
discuss
discussed
disregard
dissatisfied
distort
drawers
eagerly
eerie
effect (result)
embarrass
embarrassment

emigrate
enrol
entered
enthral
equipped
eventually
exaggerate
except
excitement
exercise
existence
experience
extremely
favourite
February
field
finally
finished
foreign
forestall
forty
friend
fulfil
furniture
gaol
gaping
gauge
glimpse
goal
government
grateful
grieved
guarantee
guard
guest
gullible
haggard
handled
harass
height

helpful
holiday
honourable
hordes
humorous
icy
illegal
imitate
immediately
immensely
impertinent
incidentally
independent
ingenious
interfere
irrelevant
irreparably
irritable
jewellery
keenness
knowledge
labour
laid (*never* layed)
leisure
lightning
likable
loneliness
loser
lovable
magazine
magnificent
manoeuvre
mantelpiece
minutes
mischievous
momentous
museum
must have
necessary
niece

ninety
noisy
noticeable
nuisance
occasion
occasional
occurred
occurrence
opportunities
ordinary
originally
paid (*never* payed)
paper
parallel
perhaps
permanently
persistent
personally
picnicking
possessive
practical
precaution
preferring
prejudice
presence
privilege
probably
procedure
proceed
procession
professional
programme
prominent
pursue
queue
quiet
quieter
receipt
received
recommend

reference
regrettable
relevant
responsibility
restaurant
rhyme
rhythm
safely
safety
scene
scheming
secretary
seize
senses
sentence
separate
Shakespeare
shining
shriek
similar

sincerely
sizable
skilful
smiling
soldier
solemn
something
souvenir
spiteful
stretched
studying
subtly
succeed
successful
superstitious
supplies
suppose
sure
surprise
suspicion

suspicious
technology
telephone
theatre
tolerant
tragedy
travelling
travels
treacherous
tries
trolleys
truly
umbrella
unnatural
unnecessary
until
usually
utmost
valleys
valuable

vandalism
vegetable
vicious
Victorian
view
village
virtuous
weather
Wednesday
weird
whereas
whether
whining
wondrous
woollen
worrying
would have
writing
yacht
yield

Make sure you know these words; they sound the same (or nearly the same) but have different meanings:

aloud/allowed
lose/loose
sole/soul
sun/son
were/where
of/off
weather/whether
laying/lying
to/too
further/farther/father
whose/who's
through/threw

its/it's
his/is
has/as
know/no
quiet/quite
are/our
bought/brought
fought/thought
over/other
their/there/they re
formally/formerly

The following are written as one word, not two:

ago	cannot	somebody
alone	downstairs	somehow
already	everybody	someone
anybody	everyone	something
anyhow	everything	sometimes
anyone	everywhere	somewhere
anything	however	today
anyway	indoors	tomorrow
anywhere	meanwhile	whereas
away	nobody	
beforehand	nowhere	

The following are written as two words, not one:

a lot (weak English)	every time	on top
all right	for example	one day
any more	for instance	so far
as though	in between	such as
as well	in case	thank you
at all	in fact	this afternoon
at once	in front	this evening
did not	no one	this morning
ever since	of course	

Warning: Above all, make sure you copy all words from the examination paper *correctly*.

SOME RULES FOR SPELLING: The spelling rules are endless, confusing and sometimes contradictory, but I have gathered the most useful together to explain the spelling of some of the words on the list. Do not depend upon rules, though. Correct spelling results from constant contact with words. There are no short cuts. Every error you make must be corrected and learned.

When you know them all, you will no longer be restricted to words of one syllable.

Note: The *vowels* are: a, e, i, o, u; all the other 21 letters of the alphabet are *consonants*.

GUIDELINES	EXAMPLES	EXCEPTIONS
(i) *'ie' and 'ei'*: 'i' before 'e' except after 'c' when the sound is 'ee'	niece, believe, field, shriek, yield, but ceiling, receipt, deceive	seize
(ii) *'-ys' and '-ies'*:		
(a) Consonant + 'y' changes to 'i' followed by 'es'	secretary: secretaries try: tries country: countries	
(b) Vowel + 'y': add 's' to the 'y'	valley: valleys trolley: trolleys chimney: chimneys	
(iii) *Prefixes*: To make a word opposite in meaning by adding 'mis-', 'dis-', 'in-', 'un-', 'ir-', or 'il-', all you do is add the prefix (that is, the syllable placed in front of the word).	dis + appear = disappear dis + satisfy = dissatisfy un + natural = unnatural il + legal = illegal	
(iv) *Words ending in mute 'e'* (a 'suffix' is the syllable placed at the end of a word):		
(a) The 'e' is normally dropped if the suffix begins with a vowel	love: lovable like: likable size: sizable excite: excitable achieve: achieving advertise: advertising	Words that have a soft 'c' or 'g', e.g. changeable, noticeable, knowledgeable

GUIDELINES	EXAMPLES	EXCEPTIONS
(b) The 'e' is normally retained if the suffix begins with a consonant	excitement achievement advertisement	argue: argument
(v) *'How' words end in '-ly'* (they answer how things were done, or how they happened or how people behaved):		
(a) Add '-ly' to the describing word	delicate: delicately eager: eagerly final: finally anxious: anxiously	due: duly true: truly whole: wholly
(b) When the descriptive word ends in a consonant + '-le', change the 'e' to 'y'	irritable: irritably noticeable: noticeably subtle: subtly	
(c) When it ends in a consonant + 'y', change the 'y' to 'i' and add '-ly'	icy: icily	
(d) When the descriptive word ends in '-ic', add '-ally'	heroic: heroically ironic: ironically emphatic: emphatically	public: publicly
(vi) *'-l' and '-ll'*: When you make a compound word with words that	full: grateful skill: skilful till: until fill: fulfil	

GUIDELINES	EXAMPLES	EXCEPTIONS
end in '-ll', the double changes to single.		
(vii) *More about '-l' and '-ll'*: When a word ends in a vowel + 'l', double the 'l' before adding a suffix.	enrol: enrolling enthral: enthralled fulfil: fulfilled jewel: jewellery	parallel: paralleled unparallel: unparalleled
But before '-ment' one 'l' only.	enthralment enrolment fulfilment	
(viii) *'-ise' or '-ize'*? If you are striving for perfection, you should use '-ize' and learn the list of about 25 exceptions, some of which are included here. You will find others in 'A Dictionary of Modern English Usage' by H. W. Fowler. However, both spellings are given in most dictionaries, including 'The Concise Oxford', so your safest plan would be to spell all verbs ending in '-ize' with '-ise'.	realize *or* realise organize *or* organise	'-ise' *only*: advertise advise despise disguise enterprise exercise supervise

GUIDELINES	EXAMPLES	EXCEPTIONS

(ix) *'-ice' or '-ise'?*

   (a) Use '-ice' for naming words or nouns

We give *advice* (noun).
We buy a *licence* (noun).
Regular *practice* is essential (noun).

   (b) Use '-ise' for doing words or verbs

Advise the young girl (verb)
License your dog (verb)
Practise your language skills (verb)

(x) *Stress or accent can help with spelling:*

If the accent falls on the last syllable, the consonant doubles before the suffix.

begin: beginning
occúr: occurred
prefér: preferred
regrét: regrettable

It doubles, too, when a one syllable word ends in a single consonant preceded by a single vowel.

glad: gladden
run: running
hop: hopping

note:
bénefit: benefiting
vísit: visiting
límit: limiting

(xi) *'-our':*

   (a) Keep the 'u' when '-our' comes at the end of the word, and when '-able' is added

labour
humour
honour: honourable
favour: favourable

Test the rule and make your own lists.

   (b) When '-ous' is added, drop the 'u'

humorous
laborious

GUIDELINES	EXAMPLES	EXCEPTIONS
(xii) *Endings*:		
'-able' and '-ible'	regrettable gullible	Collect lists of '-able' and '-ible' words, etc.
'-ance' and '-ence'	nuisance sentence	and keep testing yourself until you
'-ant' and '-ent'	relevant prominent	know which is which.
'-er', '-or' and '-ar'	banister corridor similar	
'-ary' and '-ery'	ordinary jewellery	

Sentence Construction

All skills improve with practice. English language skills are no exception, but you do have to keep working at them. The basic accomplishment for any writer is to be able to construct a sentence. Sir Winston Churchill, in his book 'My Early Life', recalled his schooldays at Harrow and wrote, 'I got into my bones the essential structure of the ordinary British sentence – which is a noble thing.'

You must have looked closely at hundreds of British sentences and listened to the sound of them as well. By now the 'essential structure' should be penetrating your bones, too.

To help you along your way here are some tips, many freely adapted from the examiners' reports, for better sentences and higher marks.

AGREEMENT:

1. '*-ing' phrases*: Make sure your '-ing' phrases relate to someone or something. When they do not, your work results in ridiculous constructions like, 'Being a small village, I knew everyone.'

    'Being a small village' is the '-ing' phrase and it certainly does *not* relate to 'I'. It does not relate to anything or anyone. That is why it is nonsense. There is more about this later under the heading 'Incomplete Parts of the Verb' (see pp. 38–9).

2. '*It' and 'this*': Use 'it' and 'this' with care. Both words must stand for someone or something or you will make a glaring error like:

    ' . she shook her head slightly and put it through the post-box slot'. Do not allow 'it' or 'this' to intrude into your work. When in doubt, leave them out.

3. This point is related to the preceding one. We all make a face and shudder when we hear a wrong note struck in music. Using the wrong construction in written English has the same jarring effect. Make sure your verbs and all other words agree in number and person.

Number means singular and plural. Do you understand first, second and third person?

(i) We use the *first person* to tell our personal experiences:

I, me, myself, my, mine	Singular
we, us, ourselves, our, ours	Plural

(ii) We relate it all to the *second person*:

you, your, yourself, your, yours	Singular
you, your, yourselves, your, yours	Plural

(iii) When we speak or write about others we use the *third person*:

he, him, himself, his, his	Singular
she, her, herself, her, hers	Singular
it, it, itself, its, its	Singular
they, them, themselves, their, theirs	Plural

Therefore, when you write from your own personal experience, you do so in the first person. If you write or speak *to* someone, you use the second person, and when you write or speak *about* others you use the third person.

Make sure your verbs and all other words agree in number and person.

4. *Third-person words:*

someone	anyone
somebody	anybody
something	anything
everyone	no one
everybody	nobody
everything	nothing
	none

When you use any of these words in a sentence, remember they are *singular third person* and use singular *third person* words to match:

he, she, it, him, his, her, himself, herself, itself. Use also singular forms of the verb. Here is an example: 'Everyone was excited and shouted himself hoarse during the match.' If you feel uncomfortable writing like that, say instead: 'The spectators were excited and shouted themselves hoarse during the match.'

5. *Some additional tips about agreement*:
  (i) 'This' and 'that' are singular; 'these' and 'those' are plural. We say 'this kind' or 'that kind' of material would be suitable for the bridesmaids' dresses but 'these kinds' or 'those kinds' of flowers. Even so, the construction is vague. It would be better to say: 'Flimsy lemon silk or lemon tones of taffeta would be suitable for the bridesmaids' dresses with posies of freesias in contrasting colours.'
  (ii) Collective nouns: (these are singular words that represent a collection of people, creatures or things – for example:

    a *flight* of swallows
    a *horde* of savages
    a *class* of pupils)

  (a) If the collective noun, as the subject of your sentence, means the group as a single unit, singular verbs and pronouns are necessary: 'The *class was* well-known for *its* generosity and *it* raised a total of fifty pounds.'
  (b) If it means the group as individual members, plural verbs and pronouns are required: 'The class were selling raffle tickets to one another to raise money.' (In other words, each individual pupil in the class was selling raffle tickets.)
  (iii) Subject and verb: Make sure there is agreement between your subject and verb. For example, you will always read 'there were six'; 'reading and writing are . . .' You must write like that, too.

Tenses

Look at the extract set for the summary about nineteenth-century railways on p. 77. It is written in the past tense. Can you find the first four verbs? They are: *had*; *revived*; *turned*; *converted*. Each one has a subject: *railways*; *injection*; *injection*; *injection* and to find it you ask who or what before the verb, like this:

1. What *had* (a permanent and far-reaching influence)?
2. What *revived* (old decayed fishing harbours)?
3. What *turned* (seaside villages into shipbuilding centres and resorts)?
4. What *converted* (tiny inland route centres into railway towns)?
These four verbs are *complete* verbs. All sentences are based on complete verbs, so it is important that you are able to recognize them. Each one has:

> person:　first, second or third
> number:　singular or plural
> tense:　　past, present or future

The passage on railways is written in the past tense because it has happened and is now history. It belongs to *yesterday. Today* is written in the present tense, and events expected to happen *tomorrow* or later are written in the future tense.

When your sentences contain more than one complete verb, you must be careful to get the sequence of tenses correct. To avoid making a muddle of this, it is best not to mix primary and historic tenses (see below). The only exception to this general rule is that primary should follow historic if the statement in the primary tense is true for ever. For example:

'The professor *told* (historic) his students that the early explorers *did not* (historic) *believe* that the world *is* (primary) round.

SEQUENCE OF TENSES: As a general rule:
Primary tenses follow one another. Primary tenses indicate present and future time.

Historic tenses follow one another. Historic tenses indicate past time. In the passage about the railways (p. 77), you can find examples of historic tenses following one another. Read from 'The poorest class of villagers' to the end of the paragraph and write down the complete verbs. Check with mine:

(labourers)	*began*	matches told (see p. 37)	
(wages)	*had risen*	,,	had told
(fares)	*had come (down)*	,,	had told
(railways)	*had offered*	,,	had told
(countrymen)	*made up*	,,	told
(quarter of a million)	*employed*	,,	told

PRIMARY AND HISTORIC TENSES

Primary (Present) tense: *Today*

		Note
I tell, we tell	I am telling, we are telling	(i) Verbs formed with 'has' and 'have' make a primary tense.
you tell, you tell	you are telling, you are telling	(ii) 'May' is primary.
he tells, they tell	he is telling, they are telling	(iii) 'Lie' is the present tense of to lie down.
she tells, they tell	she is telling, they are telling	(iv) 'Lay' is the present tense of to lay (a carpet).
I am told, etc.*	I am being told, etc.	(v) 'Awake', 'awaken' and 'wake' are present tenses.

Historic (Past) tenses: *Yesterday*

I was telling, etc.	I was being told, etc.	(i) 'Might' is historic.
I used to tell, etc.	I used to be told, etc.	(ii) 'Lay' is the past tense of 'lie'; 'lain' is the past participle.
I told, etc.	I was told, etc.	
I had told, etc.	I had been told, etc.	
I had been telling, etc.		(iii) 'Laid' is the past tense and the past participle of 'lay'.
		(iv) 'Awoke' is the past of 'awake'; 'awakened' is the past of 'awaken', 'woke' is the past of 'wake'

* 'etc.' indicates that 2nd and 3rd persons singular and plural follow in a similar way

Primary (Future) tense: Tomorrow

I shall tell, etc.	I shall be told, etc.	(i) 'Shall' is used to make the future tense for the *first person* ('I' and 'we').
I shall be telling, etc.		(ii) 'Will' is used for *second* and *third person* ('you', 'he', 'she', 'they').

Before the farm labourers could begin to enjoy the advantages of rail travel, certain actions had been completed. What were they? (a) wages had risen, and (b) fares had come down.

You can see from this example that 'had' is used with the past tense to indicate the completion of one action before another can begin. Notice it again in the next sentence. Leaving out 'had' is a common error made by candidates in their written work. To avoid this mistake remember that when you are writing in the past tense, if one event was complete before the other one began, the completed event needs 'had'.

Some of the worst errors are made by candidates who have not realized the difference between complete verbs and incomplete verbs.

INCOMPLETE PARTS OF THE VERB: In the same extract, look at 'beginning'; it is an incomplete part of the verb. There is no answer when you ask who or what beginning? It does not make sense. 'Beginning' introduces an '-ing' phrase (see pp. 9 and 33) and '-ing' phrases are always related to nouns when they are correctly used. This one is related to railways and tells us something about the railways.

Look at 'decayed'. This is an '-ed' form of the verb used to describe the harbours. It is incomplete. There is no answer when you ask who or what decayed?

Sometimes you will find '-ed' phrases functioning in the same way as '-ing' phrases. These, too, must be related to nouns. For example:

'Greeted by a crowd of excited children, the stagecoach completed its eventful journey.' The '-ed' phrase adds colour to the information about the stagecoach.

Present participles always end in '-ing'; past participles have different endings. Sometimes they end in '-ed', but there are many irregular ones. Here are a few: bound, blow, chosen, lain, left.

If you want to make an incomplete verb *complete*, use a helper like 'has' or 'have', 'was' or 'were'.

Some Final Advice about Words
1. Leave out 'actually' and 'really'.
2. Use 'even' and 'only' with care. Notice how they are used and where they are placed in printed sentences.
3. 'Altogether' means 'on the whole' or 'entirely'.
4. 'All together' means 'everyone in unison'.
5. Use 'among' (*not* 'amongst') and 'while' (*not* 'whilst').
6. Avoid using 'awful' and 'awfully' and all similar words for emphasis. Think carefully about what a word means before you use it. 'Awful' means 'full of wonder and admiration'. It suggests reverence.
7. Use 'between' for two and 'among' for three or more.
8. Avoid expressions in which you repeat yourself.
9. Remember that what you write in the Composition paper is your own point of view so do not waste time by saying so.
10. Never say 'off of'.

Look out for examples of all the matters covered in this Basic Skills section. You will find countless examples in your general reading. Notice especially the sequence of tenses, and agreement of subject and verb.

Although grammar is not mentioned by name in examinations these days, you do still have to write according to the rules, so do your best.

PRESENTATION

The examiners say: 'We are always glad to reward careful, correct and well set out work . . .' Do write *tidily* and *legibly*; there is no point in throwing away marks because the examiner cannot read your writing. Affectations like small circles instead of dots over 'i's and instead of full stops, letters that are difficult to decipher, and handwriting that slopes excessively one way or the other are all signs of poor workmanship.

Your best work, well presented, will always be rewarded.

2 Summary Writing

A summary is a shortened form of an original prose passage (it used to be called a 'précis'), written in your own words within a stated limit, and according to particular instructions. It trains you to read closely, to understand someone else's written word and to put the essence into your own words. It is well worth acquiring such a skill. You will find it useful for all kinds of reasons, especially in the future when you are at work. More immediately, it is a skill you need for your O-level examination.

SKILLS TESTED

Summary writing tests various talents:
  (i) Your ability to concentrate.
 (ii) Your powers of condensation.
(iii) Your command of vocabulary.
(iv) Your ability to select the correct information, and to re-present it in your own words.
 (v) Your skill in keeping to a word limit.
(vi) The degree of your skill shown in the completed summary; or, in other words, your workmanship.

It also tests the more basic abilities that are on trial in every part of the English examination:
  (i) Accurate spelling.
 (ii) Accurate punctuation.
(iii) Accurate vocabulary.
(iv) The harmonious arrangement of words in sentences.
 (v) The correct and pleasing arrangement of sentences in paragraphs.

A summary is written in continuous prose. Be prepared for variations in the instructions. You may be asked to reduce a prose passage to one third of its length; or you may have to deal with only a part of a passage and select particular information. *Make sure you read the instructions very carefully.*

SUMMARY AND DIRECTED WRITING

Some examiners tell you to aim your summary writing in a certain direction. For example, they may want you to write to a particular person – perhaps a friend – or to a group of people like the local council. You may be asked:

 (i) to write to convince someone about something using persuasive writing.
 (ii) to show reasoned thought or argument using logical writing.
(iii) to communicate a particular mood like sadness, or bring out a particular response like enthusiasm.

You will enjoy doing all these. It is satisfying to come to grips with a writer's ideas and to shape those ideas into your own way of thinking and writing. Directing your writing adds to the challenge and is something well within your grasp.

After all, you have been slanting your ideas orally for a long while now. How many times have you persuaded your parents to see your point of view? Or convinced a friend that your idea is an excellent one? I am sure you can think of occasions when you felt cheerful as well as times when you felt depressed. It has not been difficult to convey these differing moods to friends and relations. Think how it is done. Write as you speak and then tidy up your English so that you present the formal written language that is required.

Once you have mastered this, the formal writing will come naturally, but until it does, it is quite a sensible idea to speak your thoughts aloud and write down what you hear.

Summary writing appears on most examination papers in one form or another. The range of marks and time allocated to the question varies from board to board, but whichever examination you are taking, you will not be wasting your time if you practise this art until you are perfect. It will stand you in good stead for every examination, because you will learn to use words effectively; to expand your vocabulary; to write concisely; to produce correct and varied sentence construction in well-ordered paragraphs. In short, you will learn to use the language as a craftsman uses his material.

HOW TO TACKLE SUMMARY QUESTIONS

You would not dream of standing on a stage acting in a play if you had not learnt your lines. It is just as stupid to try to 'do' a summary if you have not understood the text. Think of the examiner as your audience and learn your lines. You do not want to give a poor performance. Here is some advice for a capable one:

1. *Concentrate*: Clear your mind of everything except the passage in front of you.
2. *Read the instructions*: Make sure you understand what you have to do. Notice what you are told and what you are asked.
3. *First reading*: Read the passage through for a general idea of its content. You may not be able to make sense of it immediately. *Do not panic*. Read the passage again.
4. *Close reading*: Concentrate your mind on the text. Read it until it makes sense. Keep calm. It will make sense if you persevere.
5. *Head your rough work* with a title that summarizes the passage.
6. *Make notes*: This is a very important stage in the work. Your notes should be clear and accurate. If you spread them out with plenty of space you will find they are more useful that way than cluttered and disorganized. You already have your main title. Find the key sentence or theme in each paragraph and use it as a sub-title. Number the points under each heading, writing each one on a new line. Use your own words. This means: *do not copy phrases and sentences but find your own way of expressing the essentials in the passage.*

   Remember that you have to get down to the bare bones, so scrap every particle of flesh. This includes illustrations, repetition, examples, anecdotes, figures of speech and quotations.

7. *Read the passage again*: Make sure you have included all the vital facts and then *put the original on one side*.

8. *Work from your notes and write your first draft*: You may find it helpful to write five words on every line spread across the page for ease of counting and altering later. Pay particular attention to your vocabulary and sentence-construction so that your rough draft is fluent and the points well organized.

9. If you are reporting – and you will be unless you have been asked for a letter – use *third person* words, and write as though everything happened *yesterday*. Third person words are: he, she, it, they; him, her, its, them; his, hers, its, theirs.

10. *Check your number of words* and adjust if necessary, so that you are within the limit allowed. Check your spelling, *especially of words used in the passage* and those in everyday use. Check your *vocabulary* and your harmonious *flow of language*.

11. *Check your draft* against the text to make certain that it is a faithful summary.

12. *Write your final copy* in careful handwriting without further reference to the original.

13. *Finally*, rule one diagonal line through all your rough work. Enter the number of words in brackets at the end of the completed summary and rule off. Be accurate when you count. The totals *are* checked.

Now let's look at a worked example, *following the tips for a capable performance* above.

Before we start, a word of warning. In spite of reminders during the course, and even in the examination rooms last year, several candidates did not bother about spelling, punctuation, clear and accurate English or legible handwriting. It is hard to believe, I know, but it happens. Please be careful. Never be satisfied with less than your best.

Example 1

2. SUMMARY AND DIRECTED WRITING (30 marks)

(*Read the instructions very carefully before beginning your work.*)

The following passage sets out some of the advantages and disadvantages of taking up sport as a career.

Imagine that you have a sixteen-year-old friend who is seriously thinking of becoming a professional sportsman or sportswoman. You know that other friends have been emphasizing the attractions of such a career.

Using only the information given in the passage, write a letter to your friend presenting the other side of the argument by putting *persuasively but accurately* the disadvantages of taking up sport as a career.

Your letter should be short, between 150 and 170 words. State the exact number of words you have used, but do not count the words in the address, the date, Dear ——, and your ending.

You should not attempt to summarise everything there is in the passage, but select from it only the material you need for your argument. *Use your own words as far as possible*, although you may retain words and expressions which cannot be accurately or economically replaced.

Use an appropriate form for a letter sent from one friend to another and write in clear, accurate English.

Sport has rapidly become an established part of the entertainments industry and the smallest detail of sportsmen's private lives is exposed by the media to public scrutiny. Top professionals are often described as 'stars' and large business interests exploit their skills. Considerable profits are made out of selling sports gear which is a replica of that used by the professionals; newspapers sell more copies if their sports coverage is good, and substantial gains can be made out of the spectators' willingness to gamble on results. The increasing demand for new talented sportsmen serves to strengthen the popular image of professional sport as a highly glamorous occupation; the jealousy shown to players who succeed and the failure-rate of young entrants are ignored by the press. Even those who reach the heights maintain their supremacy for only a relatively short period and then desperately need help to establish themselves in a new career.

It is always attractive to do something interesting and to do it as well as possible, but serious injury or an unaccountable loss of form quickly halts the progress of many a young sportsman. A handful of top professionals can afford a house in London, another in the country, and a third on the French Riviera, as well as a Rolls-Royce and a yacht in the Bahamas, but most professional players just manage to gain a bare living from their sport. Outdoor life can be delightful except when the prevalent weather conditions are rain, wind, snow, fog or ice. It is flattering to hear one's name chanted with acclaim by thousands on the terraces but crowds are fickle and soon forget, once time takes its toll of muscle and mind. Tommy Lawton, the football hero of the forties, spent his later years in poverty, forgotten by all but a small band of his closest friends.

Sportsmen at the height of their profession travel the world and visit exotic places. The English cricket team may spend its winters in Australian summers and the Wimbledon women champions may spend the year bathed in sunshine, but their own social lives are disrupted and leisure hours have to be sacrificed to hard, exhausting practice. All professional sportsmen must adhere to strict training schedules to maintain their physical fitness; their lives are devoted to keeping the body in peak condition by exhausting exercise combined with a strict regime of self-discipline and moderation in food and drink.

At an early age comes retirement. The financial rewards gained will probably not provide enough to live on for the rest of life and the early-retired sportsman has to seek a new career. He enters this fifteen years later than his contemporaries and often with not enough reputation in his sport to persuade an employer to pay him a high salary.

Perhaps, after all, it is better to remain a keen amateur.

(University of London, June 1981: 160/1)

---

1. *Concentrate*: Try not to let your mind wander until you have finished the summary.
2. *Read the instructions* very carefully. *What are we told?*
   (i) The passage sets out some of the advantages and disadvantages of taking up sport as a career.
   (ii) We have a sixteen-year-old friend who is attracted by the idea

of being a professional sportsman or sportswoman. Other friends have been highlighting the attractions of such a career.
What do we have to do?
 (i) Write a *letter* in good English and with orderly presentation (printed on the front page of the paper) to this friend highlighting the disadvantages of a professional career in sport. Is that all? No. We have further instructions:
 (ii) Use only the information given in the passage. That means *do not add any ideas of your own.*
 (iii) We must be persuasive, but accurate.
 (iv) We have a word limit of 150–170 words. We must state the exact number of words we have used, excluding the address, the date, Dear ——, and the ending.
 (v) We must use *our own* words.
Think about all that for a moment. How will you be persuasive? The glamour must be played down and the hard facts presented.
3. *First reading*: Concentrate. The instructions have prepared us for the gist of this passage. Were you able to pick out some of the disadvantages?
4. *Close reading*: Concentrate your mind on the disadvantages and read the passage again. Is it beginning to make sense?
5. *Head your rough work*: 'The disadvantages of taking up sport as a career'. The reason for a title is to focus your thinking. It is not required in the first or final draft.
6. *Make notes*: Select very carefully and concentrate on the word 'disadvantages'.

The Disadvantages of Sport as a Career

(i) *Sport is big business*
  (a) Sportsmen's lives become public property.
  (b) Sportsmen are used commercially to line the pockets of big business magnates in industry, the media and gambling.
(ii) *Sport is an insecure career*
  (a) Few reach the top and even those who do so cannot feel secure, as sudden calamity would soon put a stop to their success.
  (b) It is the exception rather than the rule for sportsmen to enjoy a life of luxury: for most a meagre living is more likely.

(c) Turning out in all weathers, sportsmen soon realize that the enchantment was only a dream. Jealousy of successful sportsmen and a high failure-rate among hopeful ones add to the disenchantment, and the insecurity.

(d) The supporters' loyalty is unreliable. Today's heroes will be forgotten tomorrow.

(iii) *The price of success*

Sportsmen have to surrender:

(a) freedom

(b) social life

(c) creature comforts

and suffer:

(d) bodily discomfort

(e) spartan training in all weathers

(iv) *Early retirement*

(a) Success is short-lived: early retirement is inevitable.

(b) Job applications have to be made without relevant experience, or sometimes even a good name in the sport.

(c) Gloomy prospects.

Read your notes again to check that the points you have made really are disadvantages.

Which of all those points shall we use? Choose the ones that you feel will be most persuasive. You are not likely to write to a friend in the same kind of language as the original passage. Watch out for the trap, though. Informal language – the kind that friends use – must be accurate and correct. The instruction is not an invitation to be careless or to use slang.

During the note-making did you understand which were the essentials? Detail about the 'sportsmen's private lives being exposed by the media' was an essential. It had to be absorbed by the reader and re-presented, so we say something like 'sportsmen's lives become public property' or, as you will see in the finished work, '... think what you'd have to give up. Would you really be prepared to sacrifice your privacy ...'

We leave out the explanation about how sportsmen are exploited by the manufacturing industries, the media and the bookmakers ('Considerable profits are made out of selling sports gear which is a replica of that used by the professionals; newspapers sell more copies if their sports coverage is good, and substantial gains can be made out of the spectators' willingness to gamble on results') and say, 'They are used commercially to line the pockets of big business magnates'.

Mention of 'a house in London, another in the country, and a third on the French Riviera, as well as a Rolls-Royce and a yacht in the Bahamas' is only an illustration of the essential that few professionals enjoy a life of luxury; and so, in the notes we jot down something like this: 'It is the exception rather than the rule for sportsmen to enjoy a life of luxury . . .' (see p. 47).

Are you beginning to understand what is an essential and what is illustration? Can you cut down to the bare bones now? Try this one, but cover up the rest of the page first: 'Tommy Lawton, the football hero of the forties, spent his later years in poverty, forgotten by all but a small band of his closest friends.' What is the relevance of that sentence?

Take the essence and put it into words of your own and you will say something like this: 'Today's heroes will be forgotten tomorrow.'

So what have you to do? All the time you are aiming to take in another writer's ideas, to absorb them and then re-express them in a style of your own. When you and I make notes our words will not be exactly the same, but I hope we shall find the same essentials. So far in this worked example we have covered the first six points (see p. 43). Now for number 7.

7 *Read the passage again*: Check that the disadvantages have been noted in an orderly way. Put the original on one side.

8. *Work from your notes*. Write the first draft. Every minute counts, so we will not waste time writing the address yet. Have a friend in mind and remember to be persuasive. Remember, too, that although a less formal style will be approved, slang and inaccurate, badly punctuated, unmelodious construction will lose you many marks.

Life	as	a	professional	sportsman
isn't	all	glamour,	you	know.
Have	you	thought	about	the
snags?	It	is	a	risky
career	and	few	reach	the
top.	Those	who	do,	enjoy
only	a	brief	spell	of
success	before	mother	nature	forces
them	into	early	retirement.	
	Unless	you	have	made a
fortune –	which	happens	only	in
exceptional	cases –	or	a	name
for	yourself,	you'll	have	to
look	for	a	second	career
without	much	in	the	way
of	prospects.	As	a	professional
sportsman,	think	what	you'd	have
to	give	up.	Would	you
really	be	prepared	to	sacrifice
your	privacy,	freedom	and	social
life,	and	to	exchange	creature
comforts	for	spartan	training?	
	Here's	a	grim	thought, too.
Sport	is	big	business;	you'd
be	a	victim	of	commercialism,
helping	to	line	the	pockets
of	wealthy	men:	your	own
would	probably	hold	only	enough
to	scrape	a	meagre	living.
If	the	roar	of	the
crowds	chanting	your	name	compels
you,	remember	that	today's	heroes
are	tomorrow's	forgotten	men!	
	Don't	you	think	you'd be
far	happier	if	you	remained
an	amateur?			(174)

9. Reported speech does not apply in letter-writing.
10. As our word limit is 170, before we write the final draft four words will have to go. I shall eliminate the colloquial 'you know' in the

first sentence, 'mother nature' can be replaced by 'age', and the final sentence can be reduced to '... far happier as an amateur?' That takes us just below the maximum allowed. We can use another couple of contractions, as we are writing in informal English. Our final total will then be 167. Check spellings, vocabulary and flow of language.

11. Check the draft.
12. Write the final copy:

> 163, North Street,
> Saltcombe,
> Somershire. SA2 8PX*
> 4th February 1984

Dear Keith,

Life as a professional sportsman isn't all glamour. Have you thought about the snags? It's a risky career and few reach the top. Those who do, enjoy only a brief spell of success before age forces them into early retirement.

Unless you've made a fortune – which happens only in exceptional cases – or a name for yourself, you'll have to look for a second career without much in the way of prospects. As a professional sportsman, think what you'd have to give up. Would you really be prepared to sacrifice your privacy, freedom and social life, and to exchange creature comforts for spartan training?

Here's a grim thought, too. Sport is big business; you'd be a victim of commercialism, helping to line the pockets of wealthy men: your own would probably hold only enough to scrape a meagre living. If the roar of the crowds chanting your name compels you, remember that today's heroes are tomorrow's forgotten men!

Don't you think you'd be far happier as an amateur?

> Best wishes,
> Yours sincerely,
> Martin

(167 words)

In directed writing, the main danger seems to be that while concentrating on the slant, candidates forget about the accuracy of the statements. Many seem to forget the instructions in their enthusiasm to persuade.

---

* Note where the address goes.

Example 2

2. SUMMARY AND DIRECTED WRITING (30 marks).

Imagine that you are a member of a fifth form which has recently discussed whether public examinations should be abolished or not. The dialogue below represents the discussion.

The Head of the school has shown interest in the fifth form's views and has asked you to write a clear report for him, in *two* paragraphs, setting out the arguments put forward in favour of:

(*a*) retaining examinations; *and*
(*b*) abolishing examinations.

Your two paragraphs should correspond to (*a*) and (*b*) above. *Use only the points made in the passage; do not add ideas of your own.* Select and arrange the arguments you need for your two paragraphs. *Write in good, clear, accurate English and use an appropriate style.* You must use your own words as far as possible; *do not copy out whole sentences or expressions. Do* **not** *name particular speakers in your report; deal only with the arguments themselves.*

Your whole report should not exceed 160 words altogether; at the end state accurately the exact number of words you have used.

Jack:	What's wrong with examinations, anyway? They give you something to work for and aim at. There wouldn't be much work done in schools if they didn't exist. I know I find it hard to work at a subject if I know there's not going to be a test on it.
Brenda:	It's all right for those who like them but it doesn't seem right to test all you've done at school for five years in a test that takes only an hour or two. What if you're not feeling well on the day and can't do your best? In any case, why should it be assumed that hundreds of candidates are at their peak on a particular day? We are all individuals; some are not yet at their best and some have passed the time when

they can produce their best work. We develop at different rates and it doesn't seem fair to examine everyone at the same time.

Sean: You can't set an examination for every individual when he thinks he's at his best. I think that if you've worked hard for five years you deserve a certificate at the end to show what standard you've reached. It makes all the effort worthwhile.

Brenda: That's typical! You're not arguing, surely, that taking an exam means that all your studying is finished for ever? Or are you? How many people ever read a book once they've left school?

Jack: Quite a few, I should say. In any case, once you do get into the big wide world you'll find it's very competitive. Competition is part of life and exams are just another kind of competition. Everyone has an equal chance to get the qualifications employers seem to want. If two boys or girls go for a job, the employer will take the one with most O-levels. And another thing, parents expect you to do your best and they're pleased when you pass your exams.

Linda: Employers are not very bright, if they rely only on examination results. Exams test only what you can remember on a particular day; they don't really test ability or intelligence and they don't prove what sort of person you are – whether you're honest or trustworthy, for example.

Jack: They can prove whether you can work hard or not.

Brenda: My dad says that working too hard for exams can damage your health. Why should we spend the best part of our lives, when we are young, studying night after night? I'd rather go to the club or disco. I want to enjoy myself and not spend every night swotting for an exam.

Sean: I don't know; preparing for an exam can be fun. I like doing Geography.

Jack: Have you ever thought that if you don't have exams employers would have to find another way of choosing their staff? Would you prefer to rely on favouritism or whom you happen to know? I'd rather have exams than rely on bribes or getting to know the right people in order to get a job.

Sean: Jack's got a point, there. At least exams are marked independently and it doesn't matter if your teacher likes you or not. I shouldn't like Old Higgins to mark my maths.

Jack: That's not what I was saying, really.

Linda: I suppose that if there were no exams, teachers and pupils wouldn't concentrate on the basic, important subjects like English and Maths – and French. There would be no point in coming to school if I had to waste my time on sports and games. Working for an exam makes you work hard and not mess about in class. I don't think my form would do any work at all, if they got rid of exams.

Brenda: Oh, no! You don't really think that exams make you work on the 'important' things, as you call them, do you? You have to do what the examiners think are important; you've no chance to study what you might really be interested in. And think of all the money exams cost and the time they waste! It wouldn't be so bad, if they really did sort out the more able from the less able. I'm not so sure they always do; think of all the famous people who have done a lot for mankind but who did badly at exams!

Jack: Brenda thinks it's a good thing to fail exams – probably because she knows she's had it and is making excuses in advance. Without any exams at all the standard of work in schools would go down and everyone would have to follow just what a particular teacher happened to be interested in. At least an exam means that we are spared having to work on hamsters in the Biology Lab. all the year round because Miss Eliot happens to think they are the most interesting creatures on earth!

Brenda: Aren't they? What are, then?

(University of London, June 1982: 160/1)

An hour is allocated for this question. Time yourself, but take as long as you need to finish the work. By the time you get to example 6 you must aim to complete within the time limit.

In this directed writing you must put yourself in the place of a fifth former who has taken part in a discussion about examinations. The Head wants a clear report of the main points put forward in favour of (a) retaining examinations and (b) abolishing examinations. You must use only the points printed in the passage. (Never add any views of your own in any kind of summary writing.)

Select the points you consider relevant and then compose an accurate and precise paragraph on each point of view. *Note again the instruction to write in good, clear, accurate English.*

You are told to use an appropriate style. For the Head of your school that means prepare a formal report in the best language you can write.

1. *Read quickly, concentrating all the time.* The same points were raised as you have heard before so that even if the words 'retaining' and 'abolishing' put you off at the beginning, the argument is so familiar that you can guess what the words mean.

   Never forget that the passages chosen can be understood with a little patience, perseverance and careful reading. No one is trying to trap you.

   On your rough work, write the heading that will direct your thoughts.

2. *Read slowly until you understand the passage.*

3. *Make your notes*: Select and reject the appropriate and inappropriate points. For example, *select* 'They give you something to work for and aim at' and *reject* 'There wouldn't be much work done in schools if they didn't exist. I know I find it hard to work at a subject if I know there's not going to be a test on it.' (The rejection contains illustrations of the essential fact in your selection.)

   Work through the extract, deciding whether the points made are new ideas or only illustrations. Select anything that provides a new view; reject everything else.

   Make clear, accurate notes expressed in your own words with useful sub-titles. Do not lose your concentration at any stage during the exercise. Check the instructions and text again to make sure you have done what is required.

4. *Write roughly*: Write your rough draft from your notes, putting five words well spread out on every other line. Check the number of words, spelling, vocabulary and fluency. Count your words accurately and do not exceed the limit. Make sure you have not missed anything. When your rough draft is the best you can produce, write your final copy in careful handwriting.

Rule a diagonal line through your rough work. Write the number of words used in brackets at the end of your summary. Rule off.

Check your notes and final copy with mine. I have tried to show you how to work from the text to the notes to the finished summary in the 'at-a-glance' table on pp. 57–9.

If you have put something in your notes that I have not put in mine, try to find a reason. Is yours an illustration or example, detail or repetition? Is it a point in favour of one or other of the arguments? If it is not, it should not be included. Look at your work critically and decide how you can improve it next time.

5. *Final copy*: Compare yours with this one:

Many fifth-formers said that they strongly favoured the retention of examinations as these provided a useful competitive training for life and allowed equality of opportunity. Pupils felt that good qualifications were not only a fitting reward for those who had worked hard, but also a standard for employers to judge by. Any alternative method of assessment might be open to suspicion. Examination courses motivated staff as well as pupils and safeguarded the curriculum. Abolishment would lower standards.

Others felt that examinations were an unfair test of ability and doubted that five years' work could be justly tested under examination conditions: they tested memory but failed to measure personality or intelligence; they did not take into account the well-being or otherwise of the candidates. Moreover, cramming harmed health and robbed pupils of pleasure in the evenings. As courses were restricted and results unreliable, examinations were a waste of time and money. Success was possible without qualifications.

(155 words)

Did you remember to write your report in two paragraphs?

'AT-A-GLANCE' TABLE FOR EXAMPLE 2

Text	*Notes*	*Summary*
They (examinations) give you something to work for and aim at ... If there were no exams, teachers and pupils wouldn't concentrate on the basic, important subjects like English and Maths – and French ... Without any exams at all the standard of work in schools would go down and everyone would have to follow just what a particular teacher happened to be interested in.	*Points in favour of retaining*: 1. Exams provide an incentive for pupils to work at worthwhile subjects. 2. Without exams standards would fall. 3. They safeguard the curriculum and prevent teachers from following their own interests.	Examination courses motivated staff as well as pupils, and safeguarded the curriculum. Abolishment would lower standards.
... if you've worked hard for five years you deserve a certificate at the end to show what standard you've reached. It makes all the effort worthwhile ... Competition is part of life and exams are just another kind of competition. Everyone has an equal chance to get the qualifications employers seem to want ... They can prove whether you can work hard or not.	4. A certificate is a fair reward for hard work over a long period; it is also a sign of staying power. 5. Good qualifications would influence a prospective employer. 6. The preparation is a training for life and allows equality of opportunity in a competitive world.	... these (examinations) provided a useful competitive training for life and allowed equality of opportunity . good qualifications were not only a fitting reward for those who had persevered and worked hard, but also a standard for employers to judge by.

Text	*Notes*	*Summary*
. . . would have to find another way of choosing their staff? Would you prefer to rely on favouritism or whom you happen to know? I'd rather have exams than rely on bribes or getting to know the right people in order to get a job.	7. The alternative would be open to suspicion. 8. An objective assessment is better than trying to rely on people's personal recommendations.	Any alternative method of assessment might be open to suspicion.
. . . it doesn't seem right to test all you've done at school for five years in a test that takes only an hour or two.	*Points in favour of abolishing*: 1. Exams are unfair tests as five years' work cannot be assessed in 2 hrs.	(Others felt that) . . . examinations were an unfair test of ability and doubted that five years' work could be tested justly under examination conditions . . .
What if you're not feeling well on the day and can't do your best? In any case, why should it be assumed that hundreds of candidates are at their peak on a particular day? . . . Exams test only what you can remember on a particular day; they don't really test ability or intelligence and they don't prove what sort of person you are – whether you're honest or trustworthy, for example.	2. Some will feel better than others on the exam day. 3. Exams make superficial assessments: they test memory, but fail to assess personality and intelligence.	They believed that examinations tested memory, but failed to measure personality or intelligence; they did not take into account the well-being or otherwise of the candidates.

Text	*Notes*	*Summary*
... working hard for exams can damage your health. Why should we spend the best part of our lives, when we are young, studying night after night? I'd rather go to the club or disco. I want to enjoy myself and not spend every night swotting for an exam.	4. Too much hard work harms your health. 5. It robs young people of the chance to enjoy their evenings.	Moreover, cramming was harmful to health and robbed young people of pleasure in the evenings.
You have to do what the examiners think are important; you've no chance to study what you might really be interested in. And think of all the money exams cost and the time they waste! It wouldn't be so bad, if they really did sort out the more able from the less able. I'm not so sure they always do; think of all the famous people who have done a lot for mankind but who did badly at exams!	6. Exams test only what examiners consider worthwhile. 7. Pupils are not encouraged to follow their particular interests. 8. They're a waste of time and money. 9. Results are unreliable. 10. Success in life need not depend upon a certificate.	As courses were restricted and results unreliable, examinations were a waste of time and money. Success was possible without qualifications.

Example 3

This paper tests your ability to read with understanding and to think about what you have read. Do not hurry. You have two* fairly long passages in front of you, but enough time for reading them. You will be wise to get to know each passage well before attempting to answer any of the questions set on it.

Remember that this is an examination in English Language. It is important not only to answer the questions correctly but also to write your answers in clear, careful English, with proper attention to spelling and punctuation.

1. Read carefully the following passage, and answer the questions set on it.

Before about 4000 BC there was no settled agriculture in Great Britain or Ireland. The inhabitants gained their living from what they could kill or gather. They hunted the wild animals, fished, snared birds, dug out insects, and ate whatever wild plants were found to be palatable, following a way of life similar to the 5 Australian aboriginals of a century ago. In some places there was an abundant supply of food throughout the year, such as by rocky coastlines where they could always be sure of finding shellfish. Inland, they moved from camp to camp, living in one place during the winter, in another in the summer, following the wanderings 10 of the animals they hunted; and they stripped the trees of nuts and fruit. They developed the technique of chipping flints until they had a wide variety of tools: axes, scrapers, knives, flint-tipped arrows, awls for boring holes in wood and bone, and even saws, and their finely shaped and barbed harpoons have been found at 15 several sites. We presume they made wooden objects too, for at Star Carr in Yorkshire an oar was discovered, and perhaps their boats were skin-covered coracles kept watertight with animal fat.

But these people had no pottery, no knowledge of cultivating the ground, and as far as we know did not domesticate animals. 20 About 4000 BC another culture arrived in these islands that could do all these things and more besides. They brought with them

* Only one passage has been used in this example.

a totally different way of life. Although they still had not discovered metals, and therefore the new culture was stone-age like its predecessor, archaeologists distinguish them by calling the earlier 25 culture the Mesolithic (Middle Stone Age) and the later one the Neolithic (New Stone Age).

The most important change was the introduction of farming, which brought with it the need to remain more or less in one place. The countryside was mainly covered with woodland, oak, 30 elm, lime, and alder, which had to be cleared by felling and burning. A primitive wheat, called emmer, was planted out for the main cereal crop, and a little barley was also grown. The people of the Mesolithic Period almost certainly lived, like the Red Indians, in transportable tents made of animal skins over a wooden frame- 35 work, but the neolithic tribes did not need to migrate in search of food; they had to be static to tend the crops. Thus settlements began, and sites of early houses are known, dating from about 3500 BC. Probably they were timber-framed, with walls made of split planking and roofs either thatched or covered with turves. 40

The new way of life did not arise spontaneously in the British Isles. Farming began in the lands around the eastern end of the Mediterranean Sea, in what is now Israel, Iran, and Asia Minor, perhaps around 7000 to 6000 BC, when the mesolithic tribes were just beginning to repopulate northern Europe. Slowly the new 45 methods spread towards the west, not by a massive migration of warlike armies, as occurred in central Europe at the end of the Roman Empire, nor by streams of settlers trekking their way across the continent like the American pioneers, but more probably by the children of each generation clearing and cultivating land just 50 a little bit further west than their family home. As the population expanded there was a need for more farming land, and so where the forest was not too thick to clear, and the land not too heavy to work, there was a slow drift towards the coast of the Atlantic.

Looking back from this distance in time it is difficult to appre- 55 ciate the enormous change that had taken place. The Neolithic Revolution, as it has been called, was a major turning-point in the history of the human race, even though it took hundreds of years, as far-reaching in its consequences as the Industrial Revolution was in the eighteenth century. For the first time men became 60 settled in particular localities; in the Near East, villages and towns

were established thousands of years before the end of the Mesolithic Period in Britain. The increasing population led also to social
organization of some sort, and men co-operated in the construction
of large earthworks, whose remains can be seen to this day. The   65
interested tourist in the twentieth century will find nothing to see
from the Mesolithic Period, but there are many impressive remains
from the Neolithic that he can locate without difficulty.

   (JOHN EDWIN WOOD, *Sun, Moon, and Standing Stones*)

   (*a*) *Stone Age Man.* Why is he so called?   [2]

   (*b*) *archaeologists distinguish them by calling the earlier
culture the Mesolithic* (lines 25–26).   [6]
            (i) What is the precise meaning of *archaeologists*?
            (ii) Suggest another word (or other words) for *culture*.

   (*c*) *The new way of life did not arise spontaneously in the
British Isles* (lines 41–42).   [6]
            (i) Explain *spontaneously*.
            (ii) By what means, according to the author, did Neo-
lithic culture spread from the Middle East to the British Isles?

   (*d*) *it is difficult to appreciate the enormous change that had
taken place* (lines 55–56). By what familiar comparison does the
author help us to envisage this enormous change?   [3]

   (*e*) *there are many impressive remains from the Neolithic that
he* (the interested tourist) *can locate without difficulty* (lines 67–68).
What form do these remains take?   [3]

   (*f*) In a paragraph of some 80–100 words compare the
Neolithic way of life, as here described, with the Mesolithic.   [20]

   (Oxford Local Examinations, June 1981: 1801/2)

   This worked example is a summary question set as part of a comprehension test. It has different instructions and a different pattern, but
the basic working method is exactly the same. For this summary we
have to produce a paragraph of 80–100 words in which we compare
the Neolithic way of life with the Mesolithic – see question (f).
   Are there any other instructions? If you said that there were not,
I am afraid you are wrong. You must remember *all the time* the addi-

tional information and instructions on the front page of the paper:

1. We have to read with understanding and think about what we have read.
2. We must not hurry. There is time to read carefully.
3. We must be wise and get to know the passage well before attempting the summary.
4. We must remember that this is an examination in English Language.
5. Our summary must be written in clear, careful English with proper attention to spelling and punctuation.

All these important points have been printed on the paper to help you to do your best.

This summary is part of a paper that lasts 1¾ hours (105 minutes). Question 1 carries 40 marks and question 2 60 marks, so you must allocate your time in that proportion. Allow 40 minutes for question 1, and 60 minutes for question 2, with 5 minutes to spare for a final check at the end. You will notice that 20 marks are allocated for the summary so you must save at least 20 minutes for it. Do not linger over questions that score only 2 or 3 marks. Use your intelligence and be guided by those numbers in brackets. They are there to help you.

This is a short summary, so select with care and have in mind all the time that you are looking for information about the differing ways of life. Reject everything else. Do be careful to spell the words in the extract carefully and notice when neolithic needs a capital letter and when it does not.

When we compare, we examine the passage to discover similarities and differences in the two ways of life described. In this extract we find the similarities are the crude skills these ancient tribes possessed. But there are striking differences which you will be able to discover for yourself.

Begin the summary (question (f)) now:

1. *Concentrate.*
2. *Obey instructions.*
3. *Read quickly first.*
4. *Read slowly* until you understand the passage.
5. *Make clear, careful notes.*

Have you remembered to write down a title that will direct your thinking?

Choose your points carefully and leave out illustrations, detail, examples, anecdotes and quotations if there are any. For example, the comparison with the Australian aboriginals is an illustration of the basic fact that the primitive mesolithic people were nomadic hunters and gatherers, so leave it out. The detail of what they made with flint is not required either, but the information that they made flint tools is.

Now finish your notes. Keep concentrating.

6. *Write roughly first.*
7. *Write neatly*, remembering all the instructions, including legible handwriting which is always expected. Do not forget to write in 'clear, careful English with proper attention to spelling and punctuation'.

   I keep repeating this to you so that it becomes part of you. It is vitally important.

   Check your notes and finished version with mine.

Prehistoric men of the Mesolithic Period led a simple, nomadic existence, pitching their tents in different places while they stalked their prey. They had developed an extensive range of flint tools but although they were able to live off the land by hunting and gathering, they were unable to till it. A radical change in this way of life was introduced by the primitive neolithic tribes who succeeded them. They had similar skills but, in addition, were farmers and, as such, needed to live in one place. They cleared forests, planted crops, tamed animals and established permanent settlements.

(98 words)

Note that *one* paragraph was requested.

'AT-A-GLANCE' TABLE FOR EXAMPLE 3

Text	*Notes*	*Summary*
The inhabitants gained their living from what they could kill or gather. They hunted the wild animals, fished, snared birds, dug out insects, and ate whatever wild plants were found to be palatable ... Inland, they moved from camp to camp, living in one place during the winter, in another in the summer, following the wanderings of the animals they hunted; and they stripped the trees of nuts and fruit.	*Mesolithic*: 1. They lived off the land. 2. They were nomadic hunters setting up camp where food supplies seemed promising.	Prehistoric men of the Mesolithic Period led a simple nomadic existence, pitching their tents in different places while they stalked their prey. ... but although they were able to live off the land by hunting and gathering ...
They developed the technique of chipping flints until they had a wide variety of tools ... but these people had ... no knowledge of cultivating the ground.	3. They made a wide range of tools by chipping flint. 4. Had not learned to cultivate the land or to farm.	They had developed an extensive range of flint tools ... ... they were unable to till it (the land).
The people of the Mesolithic Period almost certainly lived in transportable tents ...		(See first sentence above: 'pitching their tents'.)

Text

. . another culture arrived in these islands that could do all these things and more besides. They brought with them a totally different way of life.

The most important change was the introduction of farming, which brought with it the need to remain more or less in one place. The countryside was mainly covered with woodland, oak, elm, lime and alder, which had to be cleared by felling and burning. A primitive wheat . . . was planted out . . . and a little barley was also grown. . . . neolithic tribes did not need to migrate in search of food; they had to be static to tend crops. Thus settlements began . . .
(Lines 20–22 tell us that mesolithic man did not 'domesticate animals' but that their successors did.)

Notes

Neolithic:

1. Brought new skills to these islands – could also do all that mesolithic tribes had learned.

2. They were farmers.
3. This meant that settlements had to be permanent.
4. Felled trees.
5. Planted crops and tamed animals.
6. Constructed permanent dwellings.

Summary

A radical change in this way of life was introduced by the primitive neolithic tribes who succeeded them. They had similar skills but . . .

. . . in addition, were farmers, and, as such, needed to live in one place. They cleared forests, planted crops, tamed animals and established permanent settlements.

Example 4

1. Read carefully the following passage, and answer the questions set on it.

A recent police report has expressed doubts about the continued use of the traditional beat and patrol system, and deeper consideration is needed as to the possible uses to which police foot-patrols can be put if they are to form part of a flexible policing system. Nevertheless there is value to be obtained from the ability of 5
policemen on foot to hear suspicious sounds without the distractions of engine noise and see suspicious sights without having to focus most of their attention on the road ahead. They are quiet and so do not excessively advertise their presence at night, yet they are prominently visible as a deterrent during the day. They are avail- 10
able to anyone who wants to stop them to talk, or seek advice or help. At the social level, they are most obviously at one with the people they police. They can form relationships with the public as they walk amongst them. They become known as individual men and women, their personalities become known; people are able to 15
select the one police officer to whom they feel able to speak about a given problem. In return, the police officers are given information which they can feed into the system or use to solve crimes or problems in their own areas.

Provided that they are equipped with effective two-way radios, 20
they can call for aid to enable them to tackle problems that are too much for one person on foot, and can carry out inquiries in their areas when directed by radio.

Given sufficient scope and support, as well as an element of permanence, a foot-patrol officer can know the area he polices to 25
a depth impossible in any other system. His patrolling is not dictated by one-way streets or width of roads. For certain types of area, the police officer on foot-patrol is the most effective means of policing. Above all, he can stimulate social activities to prevent crime by working within the community. He can identify tensions 30
before they erupt; he can remonstrate with children, advise families and diagnose welfare problems; work of this kind cannot be done from a motor vehicle.

Yet foot-patrols are expensive in the sense that the area a man or woman can cover on foot is limited. Such patrols are open to the 35
elements and officers quickly become fatigued in very hot or very cold or wet weather.

Furthermore, the foot-patrol officer makes a very small contribution to the response of the police to emergency calls. Walking
is the least efficient of the means of moving from one place to   40
another and much of an individual's physical energy is used just
for this.

It is often said that foot-patrol duty is unpopular amongst police
officers. This is an overstatement. Some police officers would
rather walk around a beat than do duty in a motor vehicle; but there   45
are provisos. The foot-patrol officer needs to be given the responsibility for policing an area at his own discretion and not
according to a set route. The area must also be suitable for foot-
policing in that it has people in it to whom the police can talk.
Dormitory areas and factory estates do not provide interesting   50
beats because there is no one the police officer can get to know.
Densely populated city areas containing small shops, houses and
flats are ideal, yet even here there may be problems if the population contains violent elements. For this reason, it may be necessary to use policemen in pairs rather than put individuals at risk.   55
The foot-patrol police officer is always vulnerable even in relatively
passive areas and may need very urgent assistance to save him from
injury if he is involved in a skirmish. A foot-patrol system needs
a mobile support system that can give a quick response to calls for
help.   60

(R. S. BUNYARD, *Police, Organisation and Control*)

(*a*)   (i) Say what you understand by a *foot-patrol officer* (line 46).   [4]

(ii) What piece of equipment, in these days, does the author think that
a foot-patrol officer must carry?

(*b*) Choose three of the following italicized words, and give briefly the
meaning they have as used in the passage: [6]

(i) a *flexible* policing system (line 4);

(ii) do not *excessively* advertise their presence (line 9);

(iii) as a *deterrent* during the day (line 10);

(iv) is always *vulnerable* (line 56).

(*c*) In a paragraph of some 80–100 words summarize the advantages of
employing police officers on foot-patrol, as set out in lines 1–33 of the
passage.   [20]

(*d*) *The area must also be suitable for foot-policing* (lines 48–49).   [10]

In about 30–40 words indicate which kinds of area, according to the author, are most suitable for foot-policing, and which are least suitable.

(Oxford Local Examinations, November 1982: 1801/2)

Here is another worked example similar to Example 3. We have to write a paragraph of some 80–100 words that summarizes the advantages of employing police officers on foot-patrol as set out in lines 1–33 of the passage. Notice again that half the marks for question 1 are allocated to the summary section (c). That tells us it is very important.

Follow the procedure as before and work out the summary on your own. Try to complete it in twenty-five minutes.

Do not read any more of this page until you have finished Example 4.

As we have to concentrate on advantages, we can disregard the first sentence since it deals with the idea of either abandoning foot-patrols, or rethinking the way of using them effectively in a modern policing system. The advantages begin in sentence two. Lines 20–23 are more disadvantages than advantages, so those can be rejected, too. Did you notice the repetition in the passage? Thoughts are repeated in lines 10–11 and 15–17.

You were not asked to compare the advantages of the foot-patrol with the car-patrol, but to summarize the advantages of the foot-patrol. I hope that is what you did. Once again I must say *please read the instructions carefully*.

Did you recognize the illustration of an essential fact in the sentence about the policemen on foot hearing 'suspicious sounds without the distractions of engine noise . . .'? All it meant was that they could give their undivided attention to detective work.

In lines 10–11 we read, 'They are available to anyone who wants to stop them to talk . . .' That idea is developed with illustration, so once you have generalized the gist there is much to leave out.

Later, in lines 28–32, there is further need for generalization. We read that 'the police officer on foot-patrol is the most effective means of policing'. In the next two sentences we are told how. Although these sentences illustrate the statement, they are significant as far as 'advantages' are concerned. You should, therefore, express them briefly by generalization.

Policemen who pound the beat can give their undivided attention to detecting crime. This results in better policing. Their unobtrusive presence is invaluable at night: their restraining influence effective by day. Being on the spot, accepted socially and known as individuals, they are able to cope with any eventuality. Two-way relationships are established for mutual good. Given a free hand and a regular beat, the foot-patrol police, with their unrestricted movement across well-known territory, have an unique opportunity of providing an efficient service. From their vantage points within the community, they can spot the danger signals and prevent potential crime.

(100 words)

(See p. 81 for a note about the tense of this summary.)

'AT-A-GLANCE' TABLE FOR EXAMPLE 4

Text	*Notes*	*Summary*
Nevertheless there is value to be obtained from the ability of policemen on foot to hear suspicious sounds without the distractions of engine noise and see suspicious sights without having to focus most of their attention on the road ahead.	*Advantages of having P.C.s walking the beat (detection and prevention of crime):* 1. They are in a better position to give their complete attention to detecting crime.	Policemen who pound the beat can give their undivided attention to detecting crime, resulting in better policing.
They are quiet and do not excessively advertise their presence at night, yet they are prominently visible as a deterrent during the day.	2. Their unobtrusive presence is useful at night. 3. They provide an effective restraining influence by day.	Their unobtrusive presence is invaluable at night; their restraining influence effective by day.

Text	*Notes*	*Summary*
They are available to anyone who wants to stop them to talk (lines 10–11) ... (to) In return, the police officers are given information which they can feed into the system or use to solve crimes or problems in their own areas (lines 17–19).	4. They are easily available for any eventuality. 5. They know the public and are known by name. 6. Liaison between police and people is mutually beneficial.	Being on the spot, accepted socially and known as individuals, they are able to cope with any eventuality. Two-way relationships are established for the mutual good.
Given sufficient scope and support, as well as an element of permanence, a foot-patrol officer can know the area he polices to a depth impossible in any other system ... (to) ... effective means of policing (lines 28–29).	7. Foot-patrols provide a unique opportunity for comprehensive policing once a regular routine has been established. 8. Their knowledge of the territory is second to none.	Given a free hand and a regular beat, the foot-patrol police with their unrestricted movement across well-known territory have a unique opportunity of providing an efficient service.
Above all, he can stimulate social activities to prevent crimes by working within the community. He can identify tensions before they erupt; he can remonstrate with children, advise families and diagnose welfare problems.	9. Their social involvement in the community lessens the risk of crime. They recognize the danger signals and act quickly to forestall trouble.	From their vantage points within the community, they can spot the danger signals and prevent potential crime.

Example 5

1. Write a summary of the following passage in good continuous prose, using not more than 120 words. State at the end of your summary the number of words you have used. The passage contains 345 words.

(16 marks)

Navvies were not newcomers to the English scene. For many years villages near canal workings had seen young men go off with the navvy gangs, as lost to home and friends as those who took the King's shilling. Over the years there had grown up a caste of specialized nomad labourers with their own habits and traditions; and although the railway boom vastly increased their numbers and spread them to every region of the country, it did not destroy their sense of being a race apart. Moreover, the huge forces of them now recruited enabled the railway navvies to be as much a law to their truculent selves as their eighteenth-century predecessors, so that inhabitants of districts where large-scale construction works were in hand found themselves living under a sporadic reign of terror, made supportable only by the long hours the navvies worked. Quiet villages, where the law was represented by a part-time parish constable, would be invaded by a horde of brawny, insolent men in strapped velveteens and spotted neckcloths, inclined to spend their leisure lounging about the lanes, accosting local women, taunting their menfolk and generally spoiling for trouble. Cottagers, farmers and landowners all suffered, for navvies would pillage orchards and hen-roosts like an army of occupation, and they were ardent poachers.

It was not only rural parishes that felt the weight of the navvy's hand. Of an evening, when work on a nearby railroad was over for the day, chance passers through a country town might find the place apparently deserted by all respectable citizens; they had retired indoors leaving the streets to the navvies and their hangers-on. In fact, where they were in strength, the railway navvies seem to have held the local authorities in contempt.

But there were compensations. Experienced, fully able navvies might get about twice the current wage of ordinary labourers and, since they were notoriously free spenders, they were not altogether unwelcome to butchers, bakers and brewers. They crammed themselves into any lodging they could find, and for all their destructiveness were likely to be profitable tenants.

KELLOW CHESNEY

(Associated Examining Board, June 1979: 025/2)

Examples 5 and 6 are different again. This time the paper includes a summary question (16 marks), a comprehension test (20 marks) and two further questions (carrying 8 and 6 marks). The time allowed is 1¾ hours (105 minutes) so you should allocate your time as follows:

Question 1: Summary – 35 minutes
Question 2: Comprehension Test – 40 minutes
Question 3: Usage – 15 minutes
Question 4: Usage – 10 minutes

That leaves 5 minutes for a final check.

The instructions this time state that we are required to write a summary in 'good continuous prose' and we have to do this using not more than 120 words. 'Good continuous prose' is the kind of writing that sounds correct when it is read out aloud. Naturally, you cannot apply this kind of test in an examination room, but while you are studying, it is a sensible idea to read out your work from time to time. In any case, *always* listen with your inward ear to test for harmonious flow and pleasing sound. Another word for this is fluency.

Read no further until you have completed the summary.

Did you pick up the gist of the passage after the first reading or were you immediately put off by some words that you had not come across before? I hope you remembered what I said earlier: you may not be able to make sense of a passage immediately. *Do not panic.*

You may not have heard the word 'navvy' before. What were you supposed to do? Read on and keep on reading. Look for clues. It should not have been long before you were able to make an intelligent guess. You would not be allowed to have a dictionary with you during the examination so you should do your best to make sense of the passage without reference to one during the practices.

By the time you had finished the close reading, and kept calm you should have discovered that the passage was about labourers and the effect they had on rural life when extensive construction work was underway.

Is that what you discovered? I hope you persevered with this one, for you would have realized that your first impression was unreliable. If the 'King's shilling' worried you at first, for example, you can see how unimportant it actually was.

Next time you read a passage that seems difficult, remember that the examiners know what you are capable of understanding and they set the papers accordingly. No one is trying to catch you out. If you read the text carefully, you will always be able to make sense of it.

This particular summary was more difficult than most because it contained several unfamiliar words. However, by concentrating your whole mind upon it and reading and re-reading, you should have found the essence and been able to re-present it just as you have done in other summaries.

Did you notice that you were not told specifically to use your own words but, even so, you would be wise to stick to the method we have been practising. The best summaries are always produced by candidates who are able to take in the essentials of the original, and who can find their own way of expressing them in precise and coherent language. As we have no instructions about numbers of paragraphs, it is advisable to follow the pattern of the original.

Travelling navvies have recruited local youth, established a crude code of behaviour and set themselves apart from other workers since the eighteenth century. In spite of increased numbers and extended working areas, railway navvies continued in the same tradition. They swarmed aggressively into local villages, terrorizing and overwhelming the people, stealing their livelihood and provoking trouble.

Inhabitants of nearby towns did not escape either and stayed indoors when gangs of navvies invaded, threatening violence and defying the law.

On the credit side, it must be said that they were well paid and eager to spend their wages. Traders and landlords benefited from their stay, despite the damage the navvies had done.

(111 words)

N.B. Vandalism is an overworked word used incorrectly today – resist the temptation to use it in this summary.

'AT-A-GLANCE' TABLE FOR EXAMPLE 5

Text	*Notes*	*Summary*
Navvies were not newcomers to the English scene. For many years villages near canal workings had seen young men go off with the navvy gangs ... Over the years there had grown up a caste of specialized nomad labourers with their own habits and traditions;	*Exclusive class of specialized nomad labourers – their effect on village life:* 1. Navvies date from eighteenth century. 2. Have always recruited local youth and established a crude code of behaviour.	Travelling navvies have recruited local youth, established a crude code of behaviour and set themselves apart from other workers since the eighteenth century.
and although the railway boom vastly increased their numbers and spread them to every region of the country, it did not destroy their sense of being a race apart. Moreover the huge forces ... (to) ardent poachers.	3. Number increased with the growth of railways. This did not alter their exclusiveness, and they were as ruthless as their predecessors.	In spite of increased numbers and extended working areas, railway navvies continued in the same tradition.
	4. Villagers were terrorized. Their livelihood stolen. Their peace threatened. (They could bear it only because the invasions were short-lived.*)	They swarmed aggressively into local villages, terrorizing and overwhelming the people, stealing their livelihood and provoking trouble

---

* It was necessary to cut the notes so this point was omitted on the grounds that it does not relate to the main heading.

Text	*Notes*	*Summary*
Paragraph 2	*Their effect on towns:* 5. There was no escape here either. 6. Law-abiding citizens were forced to stay indoors while gangs of navvies defied the authorities.	Inhabitants of nearby towns did not escape either and stayed indoors when gangs of navvies invaded, threatening violence and defying the law.
Paragraph 3	*Compensations:* 7. Navvies were well paid for their work. 8. They enjoyed spending their money. 9. Traders and landlords benefited from their custom, despite their destructiveness.	On the credit side it must be said that they were well paid and eager to spend their wages. Traders and landlords benefited from their stay despite the damage the navvies had done.

Example 6

1. Write a summary of the following passage in good continuous prose, using not more than 120 words. State at the end of your summary the number of words you have used. The passage contains 350 words. (16 marks)

The railways, beginning in earnest in the 1830s, had a permanent and far-reaching influence on village life. Their life-giving injection of cheap and rapid transport revived old decayed fishing harbours like Grimsby, turned seaside villages into shipbuilding centres and resorts, like Barrow-in-Furness and Southend, converted tiny inland route centres into railway towns, the home of engine works, like Crewe, Swindon, Wolverhampton, Norwich, Worcester and Ashford. The scenery itself was changed. To secure the easy gradients demanded by railway engineers great embankments and high viaducts were thrown across wide valleys, soaring bridges made light of deep river barriers, and tunnels, their portals massively decorated with turrets and battlements, penetrated steep hillsides. Little hamlets of railwaymen grew up around the stations, which were generally a mile or two from the centre of the villages they served. These new communities were related to existing villages, because railways served as major outlets for farm commodities and as a means of obtaining supplies of fertilizer and farm equipment. Slow passenger trains, stopping at country halts, provided a new, and eventually cheap, way of getting to market towns, and there was the occasional excursion trip to the seaside or beauty spot. The poorest class of villagers, however, the farm labourers, began to enjoy the advantages of railway travel only towards the end of the century, when wages had risen and the fares had come down. But long before this the railways had offered the village lads a more attractive means of employment, and country men made up a fair proportion of the quarter of a million employed by the railways in the 1870s.

Though railways offered a new field of employment, they also destroyed an old one. The advent of cheap, fast railway travel spelled the early demise of the coaches. Within a few years it was no longer possible for the roadside cottager to set his clock by the passing of the mail, or for country children to wait excitedly for the great event of the stage's appearance, emerging suddenly over the brow of the hill with whip cracking and steam rising from the horses.

G. E. MINGAY

(Associated Examining Board, June 1980: 025/2)

This summary is like Example 5, so you should be able to complete it in 35 minutes. Apply everything that you have learned about summary writing to this one and see what you can make of it.

You were not tempted to name names of the places revitalized by the railways, I hope? Those names added *detail* to the basic fact that cheap and quick transport injected new life into run-down villages.

How did you fare in trying to condense the ideas contained in the third and fourth sentences? Embankments, viaducts, bridges and tunnels were all *examples* of massive organized structures. Some candidates would be tempted to mention two of the examples but would happily leave out the other two. If one is mentioned, all must be mentioned so that you avoid the pitfall of unequal compression of ideas. If you tried to leave all four in your summary you would soon discover that you had too many words. That should guide you to the conclusion that you must generalize sentence four.

The last sentence is an illustration of the fact that the stagecoach era is over.

Illustrations, examples and *detail* have no place in summary writing. If anything significant is included in the illustration, express it briefly by generalization.

Railways, begun in 1830, made a lasting impact on village life. They deformed for ever the natural face of the countryside as vast construction works ruthlessly prepared the land for the network. Villages and towns were linked by the main line and, thus revitalized, became important centres for industry and tourism. Communities of railwaymen, attracted by the job prospects, grew up around the stations providing local villages with a quick and cheap goods and passenger service, the latter offering a new sense of mobility to the villagers. The poorest class had to wait forty years before it could afford the same facilities.

Once the railways' success was assured, it was not long before coaches became redundant.

(116 words)

'AT-A-GLANCE' TABLE FOR EXAMPLE 6

Text	Notes	Summary
The railways, beginning in earnest in the 1830s, had a permanent and far-reaching influence on village life. Their life-giving injection of cheap and rapid transport revived ... (to) Ashford.	*The lasting influence of the railways on rural life:* 1. Railways' lasting impact began in 1830. *Effect on towns and villages:* 2. They put new life into run-down villages, with their cheap and quick transport. 3. They promoted small inland towns so that they became important centres of industry.	Railways, begun in 1830, made a lasting impact on village life. ... providing the local village with a quick and cheap goods and passenger service ... Villages and towns were linked by the main line and, thus revitalized, became important centres for industry and tourism.
The scenery itself was changed. To secure the easy gradients demanded by railway engineers great embankments and high viaducts were thrown across wide valleys, soaring bridges made light of deep river barriers, and tunnels, their portals massively decorated with turrets and battlements, penetrated steel hillsides.	*Effect on landscape:* 4. Massive engineering works deformed the countryside as preparations were made for the network.	They deformed, for ever, the natural face of the countryside as vast construction works ruthlessly prepared the land for the network.

Text	*Notes*	*Summary*
Little hamlets of railwaymen ... (to) in the 1870s.	*Effect on people:*	
	5. Railwaymen formed communities around the stations built just outside the villages.	Communities of railwaymen, attracted by the job prospects, grew up round the stations providing local villages with a quick and cheap goods and passenger service, the latter offering a new sense of mobility to the villagers. The poorest class had to wait forty years before it could afford the same facilities.
	6. Many, including locals, had joined, attracted by the employment prospects.	
	7. Goods in and out of the district were sent by train.	
	8 Villagers enjoyed a new sense of mobility.	
	9. Poorest class had to wait about forty years before it could enjoy the same freedom.	
Last paragraph.	10. The success of the railways resulted in the failure of their predecessors	Once the railways' success was assured, it was not long before coaches became redundant.

FINAL THOUGHTS
ABOUT SUMMARY WRITING

On p. 44 I mentioned that unless you were writing a letter you should use *third person* words and write as though everything happened *yesterday* – in the *past tense*. This is a rule from the old précis and on the whole is good advice, but now and again you will find yourself wondering whether or not it would be more appropriate to write in the present tense. A case in point is our fourth worked example in which we had to summarize the advantages of employing police officers on foot-patrol. Did you find yourself automatically using the present tense?

It is not difficult to see a reason for this. The passage discusses an up-to-date problem, and when this happens it is natural – and acceptable to examiners – to condense in the present tense.

The second worked example also contains a present-day problem, but for that one we had to write a report on a discussion that had already taken place, so I chose the *third person* and the *past tense*. You would not have been wrong if you had used the present tense for that one.

The examiners say the present tense will be appropriate for reducing passages that deal with current problems, but that the past tense will be expected otherwise.

Finally: some boards in their instructions to candidates at the beginning of a summary question say 'in your own words' and some do not. Please remember that the best summaries are those that condense the essence of the passage. This cannot be stressed too often. The best work is always that which is absorbed and then re-expressed in the candidate's personal style.

Good summaries are evidence of good understanding. They can never be produced by stringing together some of the writer's words and phrases, or by twisting yourself into a knot to find another word for a spade. Believe it or not, that has been done and a candidate has written about 'a garden tool for digging'. Others have invented different ways of saying railways, examination, sport – the list is endless.

3 Comprehension

A comprehension test is a series of questions designed to discover how well you respond to the printed word.

Like summary writing, a comprehension test trains you to read closely and to understand someone else's ideas and expression.

SKILLS TESTED

Written Comprehension
In addition to the basic skills on trial throughout the examination the written comprehension tests:

   (i) Your ability to concentrate.
   (ii) Your ability to read closely.
   (iii) Your ability to discriminate (to see the difference between; to choose carefully).
   (iv) Your understanding of usage including idiom and figurative language.
   (v) Your power to think about and understand the written word.
   (vi) Your ability to draw conclusions as a result of what you read.
   (vii) Your appreciation of a writer's style.
   (viii) Your workmanship in presenting your answers in your own words and with pleasing arrangement.

Multiple-choice Comprehension
The skills being tested in multiple-choice tests are the same as those listed above, but you can devote all your time to thinking and under-

standing without having to worry about composing coherent answers in your own words.

Make sure you understand these words:

'except':   leave out, exclude; apart from
'inferred': gathered, reasoned, deduced
'implied': hinted, suggested

They are freely used in multiple-choice tests.

Answers have to be selected from four or five options and each answer marked clearly on a special answer sheet. You work in pencil, marking your answer sheet according to the board's instructions, and then it is corrected by computer.

EXAMINERS' WORDS OF WARNING

1. Spell words that have been printed on the examination paper correctly.
2. Read words carefully. There is too much mis-reading which leads to misunderstanding.
3. Vague answers do not score points.
4. Comprehension is not a test of your ability to copy sentences from the question paper on to your answer sheet!
5. Make sure you include all that is relevant when writing your answer. A common mistake is to refer to part of the text and to ignore another part that contains a vital point. This kind of error is the result of superficial reading.
6. Answers are often too long-winded and include irrelevant material. Answer the question and then stop. But check that you have given a complete answer. If the question is in two or three parts, do not forget part two when you have finished part one.
7. Look at the mark allocated for each answer and plan accordingly.
8. *Obey instructions:*
    (i) If you are asked to *supply* a *word* or a *phrase* for *three* of the following four expressions, *do exactly that.*
    (ii) If you are asked to *quote* a *word, phrase* or *sentence, do exactly that* and remember the inverted commas.

(iii) If you are not specifically (especially) asked for either of the above or anything similar, *answer in sentence form* and *use your own words*: it is always better to re-express what you read in your own style. It is more rewarding for you and tells the examiners that you are one of the better candidates.

Now we shall look more closely at the skills being tested:

 (i) *Concentration*: Nothing worthwhile will be achieved unless you direct your thinking as you did for summary Once your mind wanders you reduce your chance of success.

 (ii) *Close reading*: The more you read the passage, the clearer it becomes. You should read it at least twice before you pick up a pen or pencil. During the third reading – which includes reading the questions – jot down some rough notes.

(iii) *Discrimination*: When you discriminate you make a careful, well-considered choice. Many of the multiple-choice questions ask, 'Which one of the following words is closest in meaning to "____" as used in line ____?' Written comprehension asks similar questions, only you have to provide the answer from your own vocabulary. It is important that the word or definition you give can be used in the original without altering the sense. Another kind of discrimination is selecting the relevant and rejecting the irrelevant subject-matter. The clue to being relevant is printed in the question. Answer *exactly* what you are asked. Choose carefully.

(iv) *Usage, idiom and figurative language*:
 (a) Some boards include a question that tests your understanding of basic English Language skills. For example, you may be asked to explain the use of a colon or an apostrophe 's' (see pp. 15 and 19).
 (b) When you write about figurative language, always ask yourself what difference it has made to your understanding of the passage. How effective or appropriate is the image created? Often the figure will be a simile or metaphor in which an author highlights an aspect of similarity between two dissimilar things. Take, for example, 'The road through the town was polished like

porcelain.' The writer has picked an aspect of similarity between the icy road and polished porcelain. When they are compared, the glazed, translucent surface is the shared quality and thus the porcelain creates an appropriate image, enabling the reader to visualize the slippery, shiny road.

Literary work abounds in images, pictures that you can see with your 'inward eye'. Their purpose is to make the writer's meaning clearer and more vivid.

(v) *Thinking about and understanding the written word*: This is the main purpose of comprehension. Once you have understood the passage, you should be able to answer most of the questions without difficulty because the information you need is printed there in front of you. Remember that sometimes relevant facts are at the end of the passage, so if you do not read it through several times before you begin to answer, you will make careless mistakes.

(vi) *Drawing conclusions from the printed word*: Comprehension tests more than the direct meaning of a text. It tests your ability to discover what lies below the surface. Words used for this kind of question include: deduce, infer, gather, draw, conclude, derive; and words made from these like deduction, inference and so on.

To answer well, you must look for clues and think about meaning all the time. For example, look at lines 10–19 in the extract on pp. 90–91. What inferences can we draw about Miss Jameson from her reactions to Sarah's proposal? We can infer that she is deputy headmistress. The clue here is that the headmistress sent for her to tell her about the revised arrangements for the afternoon. We can infer that she has held this position for some time. Did you spot the clue? Miss Jameson compared Sarah's decision with the way Miss Holmes would have acted. We can safely assume that Miss Jameson was Miss Holmes's deputy first, and that Miss Holmes was Sarah's predecessor. We can infer that Miss Jameson preferred the old regime.

It is not too difficult: look for the clues and think about

what you are reading. Make sure you understand what the question is asking you. Weigh up the arguments, for and against, if appropriate, and then draw your conclusions.

(vii) *Style*: All writers have style. It is the way they express themselves: how they use words and imagery; how they construct their sentences; how the detail of their writing adds to the general effect; their tone; the atmosphere created; the kinds of things they write about; the register (form of language) they use for their work.

By studying style you can gather (inference again) several facts about writers, including their attitude to their subjects, their feelings about it, their intended audience, and their main purpose in writing.

Sometimes you may be able to deduce their approximate age; the part of the country they come from; their politics, religion or philosophy; and a variety of other details that make all writers what they are.

You may or may not be asked a question to test your knowledge of style. If you are, you must decide how the author's style is appropriate to his or her text and how he or she is communicating to you, the reader.

While on the subject of style, think about your own. Style is personal. It is as much a part of you as your room at home, or the clothes you wear. We shall look into this in our next section, but meanwhile learn all that you can from the experts.

(viii) *Workmanship*: Workmanship is the means through which you advertise yourself. You reveal your attitude in the way you arrange your work and in the way you set about it. You are judged by how well you have read the passage; how well you prepare your answers; how well you write them down.

As you work through the examples take note of the arrangement of the answers. Your guideline is quite simple: make your answers clear, numbering carefully to match the question paper and presenting them in an orderly fashion.

HOW TO TACKLE COMPREHENSION QUESTIONS

As you prepared for summary writing (p. 43), so you must prepare for comprehension. To give a splendid performance, learn your lines and please your audience.

1. *Concentrate*: Clear your mind of everything except the passage in front of you.
2. *Read the instructions.*
3. *Work out how much time you have* and which questions carry most marks.
4. *First reading*: Read straight through the extract, taking in what you can but without worrying too much. Keep calm if it seems hard. You have plenty of time to read it until it makes sense.
5. *Close reading*: Read and re-read until you can understand the passage as a whole. Read through the questions, too, if it is a traditional comprehension.
6. (i) *Written comprehension test*: Read the questions one at a time and think about what you are being asked to do in each. Work in rough, composing your response in clear, accurate English. Keep an eye on the time and allow sufficient to write out your answers neatly in readable handwriting. As you answer each question, check the original to make sure you have included everything that is relevant; check, too, that you have not included material that is off the point, or irrelevant.

   (ii) *Multiple-choice test*: Answer the questions one at a time and work steadily through the paper. There is no advantage to be gained in reading all the questions before you begin the first one, so do not waste time by doing so. *Read each question carefully, as you come to it.* Mark your answer sheet with a clear, firm, black line. See pp. 83 and 107 for further advice about multiple-choice questions.
7. Do not linger over any question that seems difficult. Leave it out for the time being, and work on. Finish the paper, and then return to the difficult ones, doing the best you can with them. Number your answers to match the numbers on the question paper. It is best to work through in sequence, but if you have to leave anything

out, you are allowed to add that question (or questions) after you have answered the bulk of the paper. It is better to do that than to leave a space, because you will not know how much space you will want.

9. Rule out your rough work with a neat diagonal line.
10. Rule off your completed answer.

Written Comprehension Test Examples

TRIAL EXAMPLE

Return to the passage we used for summary in Example 3 on p. 60. On that occasion we worked out the time allocation and decided we had 20 minutes for the comprehension. See what you can do in 20 minutes. Do not look at my answers until your 20 minutes are up. First, though, a word about the answers that I shall be giving you throughout the worked examples section. If your answers do not match mine exactly in the written comprehension it does not mean you are wrong. We shall both be making personal responses to the questions and therefore we shall not answer in carbon-copy style.

Look on the answers as suggestions or guidelines. If you find that you are saying the same kinds of things in different words, then your answers will be correct. Remember that you must be concise and that marks are lost if you ramble. The quality of your written expression will be diluted.

1. (a) 'Stone Age Man' is so called because stone implements were a feature of his culture.
   (b) (i) Specialists who study the remains of prehistoric cultures are called 'archaeologists'.
       (ii) Stage in human development.
   (c) (i) 'spontaneously': The word 'spontaneously' means 'instinctively'. The new way of life did not develop instinctively, but evolved as a result of outside influence.
       (ii) The Neolithic culture from the continent evolved very slowly indeed. It seems likely that each succeeding generation cleared and cultivated a little more of the land, extending family territories further towards the west until, in time, Neolithic influence had crossed the whole British Isles.
   (d) To help us to appreciate the enormous change that had taken place, the author likens the Neolithic Revolution to the Industrial Revolution of

the eighteenth century Each had a profound effect on man's progress.

(e) The 'impressive remains from the Neolithic that he can locate ...' take the form of large earthworks and sites of early settlements

Now check your answers:

(a) Did you remember the inverted commas and capital letters for 'Stone Age Man'?

(b) (i) Did you spell 'archaeologists' correctly? Did you give a precise definition? If you say they are 'specialists' that is more precise than saying 'men'; if you say 'they study the remains of prehistoric cultures' that is more precise than saying 'they dig up the past'. We can use the word 'culture' because the next question asks us to define it.

(ii) Notice that this time we are asked for a 'word (or other words)' *and that is all.*

(c) (i) 'Explain' is an instruction to answer in your own words and to show that you understand the word *as it is used in the passage.*

(ii) Do not fall into the trap of long-windedness. Did you think out a clear sentence or two before you wrote your answer? If you used the word 'Britain' or 'Britons' did you spell them correctly, and 'author', which is printed on the paper?

(d) When you comment on the comparison you must say how it helped us to 'envisage the enormous change'. Both revolutions were turning points in history and, as such, had a profound effect on man's progress.

(e) This one is straightforward.

Example 1

---

55 minutes allowed

The use of dictionaries in this examination is prohibited.

Read the passage carefully and answer the questions that follow.

It was February when the great snow-storm came. For a day and a night snow smothered the South Riding. Drifts blew across the bleak stretches of Cold Harbour Colony, burying by

the dozen the huddled sheep. The Council Library van, blinded
by the blizzard, was abandoned in a blocked ditch outside   5
North Wirral, the driver barely escaping with his life. All
Wednesday and Thursday the storm raged and blustered. By
Friday its fury had subsided; a sullen sun gleamed from the
ashen sky on to a transfigured landscape.

Sarah* sent for Miss Jameson and told her that such   10
dramatic weather was too rare to waste in classrooms.

"The girls may never see anything like it again. It will be an
experience to remember long after, perhaps, they've forgotten
all that we can teach them. We won't have any afternoon classes.
Ask Miss Becker to come and see me, will you?"   15

Miss Jameson disapproved of Miss Burton's sudden decision
to turn an afternoon's timetable upside-down. Not thus had
Miss Holmes acted. But since the arrangement meant more
leisure for herself she made no protest.

The plan was that Miss Becker and two of the senior girls   20
should set off on a route known to themselves and Sarah alone.
Ten minutes later the others should follow their trail, wherever
it might lead.

It was nearly three o'clock when Sarah set off in her car to
an appointed rendezvous with the runners on Maythorpe cliffs.   25
The road through the town was polished like white porcelain.
A wild wind blew the seagulls about the esplanade, wheeling
and shrieking. Her hands tightened on the wheel as she swung
her car past a lumbering bus and off the main road south to
Maythorpe village. A gate to a field towards the cliffs was open.   30
Scuttering and slithering over the rutted snow, she passed
through three open gateways, and found herself right on the
edge of the cliff, where, sure enough, according to plan, she saw
the track of the "hares" leading down a slope where the earth
had fallen on to the snow-covered shore. There she waited,   35
hanging, it seemed, suspended between the white frozen earth
and black tumbling sea.

An extraordinary scene she found it, a reversal of natural
colour. White snow shrouded the sands and piled against the
cliff; but the retreating tide stained its shining surface with huge   40
black semicircles; the water was black; the sombre sky was

---

* Sarah Burton is the headmistress of the school.

ashen. The sun hung like a painted circle in a child's landscape giving no obvious illumination. All light came from the white, transforming snow.

Sarah saw the first of the girls come laughing and panting 45
and calling across the field. They cheered her as they plunged off down the slope, falling into drifts, scrambling out again, galloping away far below her, over snow-covered sand.

"Do you know you are trespassing?"

She spun round at the question, to face a big dark man on 50
a big dark horse towering above her from a bank of snow. She gasped and stared. Then her temperamental resilience re-asserted itself.

"Am I trespassing? The gates were open, and I thought that this was the usual road to the cliffs." 55

"It's not you so much," he admitted. "It's those girls— breaking down fences, scaring what ewes are left alive. There's a gate left open in the forty acre."

"But we didn't come that way."

"My neighbour has lost close on forty sheep. My tenant on 60
this farm has lost a cow in calf. They're skinning sheep as they dig them out along Cold Harbour. And this is the time you choose to let your young women career over the farms. As though it was fun, this snow."

Fun was just what she had thought it. What she did think 65
it. She was furious with him for spoiling her lovely carnival and furious with herself for her failure of imagination.

"I will take all responsibility," she said proudly. "If any damage has been done, we will of course pay compensation."

WINIFRED HOLTBY

(a) The Council Library van was "blinded by the blizzard" (lines 4–5).
   (i) Explain what this means.
   (ii) What were the consequences of this?   *(3 marks)*

(b) To what does the writer compare the storm in the last two sentences of the first paragraph?   *(1 mark)*

(c) Give the meaning of the following sentence without using the words in italics: "a *sullen* sun gleamed from the *ashen* sky on to a *transfigured* landscape" (lines 8–9).   *(3 marks)*

(d) Explain why Sarah decided to "turn an afternoon's timetable upside-down" (line 17).   *(3 marks)*

(e) Using your own words as far as possible, explain Miss Jameson's reactions to Sarah's proposal. (*4 marks*)

(f) What does the writer mean when she describes the road as "polished like white porcelain" (line 26)? (*2 marks*)

(g) Why is the word "hares" (line 34) in inverted commas? (*1 mark*)

(h) What did Sarah find extraordinary about the scene from the cliff-top? (*3 marks*)

(i) When the horseman accused Sarah of trespassing, what had really angered him? (*2 marks*)

(j) Explain Sarah's feelings at the end of this episode. (*3 marks*)

(Associated Examining Board, November 1981: 069/3)

We shall follow the guidelines set out on p. 88.

Before you start, another word of warning. Every year many hundreds of candidates rush into answering the questions before they have done more than skim through the passage. Cultivate sensible habits now so that when the time comes you will be well prepared and able to take it all in your stride.

We shall work through the first comprehension together, and then I shall leave you to do the others on your own.

1. *Concentrate*: Direct all your thinking on to the passage. We are starting with a text that you have seen before, but you will be surprised by how much more there is to learn from it.

2. *Read the instructions*: These are straightforward: 'Read the passage carefully and answer the questions that follow.' Do not forget that there will be instructions in the questions, too.

3. *Work out how much time you have.* Allow 50 minutes and that will leave you a clear 5 minutes to read through the finished paper. Take 25 minutes to read, understand and work out your answers in rough, with a spare 5 minutes in case you need it. That is 30 minutes altogether. Write out the neat answers, taking 20 minutes, and read the paper through in the final 5 minutes.

4. *First reading*: Refresh your memory by reading the extract through quickly.

5 *Close reading*: Read it slowly until the passage makes sense as a whole. Read the questions, too.

Here are some possible answers:

(a) [Think about what this question is asking you. 'Explain' means that you have to put the phrase 'blinded by the blizzard' into your own words. In part ii you must say what the consequences were. Note that 'consequences' is plural.]

   (i) 'blinded by the blizzard'. Its windscreen and windows were thick with snow so that the driver could not see to drive.

   (ii) The driver had skidded off the road and left his vehicle in a ditch.
[When *you* do this you should try to leave a line between each complete answer.]

(b) The writer compares the storm to an angry, bad-tempered person indulging in a display of temper. [The words 'raged', 'fury' and 'sullen' are the clues that lead you to this answer.]

(c) The sun was gloomy and seemed reluctant to gleam from the grey sky on to the changed landscape. [It seems that the sun was sulking and that the little glow of light that it shed was all it could manage. The question tells us specifically not to use the three italicized words, so we can presume that we shall not be penalized if we use any of the others. 'Sullen' suggests that the sun was moody and therefore reluctant to shine. You could have used 'sulky' for 'sullen' and 'colourless' for 'ashen'.]

(d) Sarah decided to 'turn an afternoon's timetable upside-down' because the impressive weather was an education in itself, and too good an opportunity to miss. She believed that the experience of the blizzard would become a lifelong memory for the pupils and that they might never see such a sight again.

(e) Miss Jameson strongly objected to the headmistress's decision to disorganize the timetable, reflecting that the previous headmistress would not have done so. However, considering that she would have some free time, she kept her objections to herself. [Notice the ' 's' after the double 's'. This question tests your knowledge of the idiom, 'upside-down'; your understanding, and your ability to draw inferences. You infer that Miss Holmes was the previous headmistress. You understand why Miss Jameson reacted as she did.]

(f) 'polished like white porcelain' contains a simile that compares the state of the road to the glazed surface of white porcelain. [It is not difficult to imagine the shiny, slippery, glazed surface of the snow-packed, icy road once the word 'porcelain' has been mentioned. It is powerfully effective and visually magnificent. This word-picture conjures up exactly the right image, making the writing vivid and real.]

(g) The inverted commas denote that the word 'hares' is not to be taken literally. It directs our minds to the thought that the advance party had laid a trail.

(h) The scene was extraordinary because light came not from the sun in the colourless sky, but from the snow which covered the beach and drifted against the cliffs. This reflected light had a strange effect that turned the sea black and changed all normal colour.

(i) The horseman was angry that thoughtless girls had left his gates open, shown no respect for his property and frightened his few surviving ewes.

(j) At the end of the episode it is clear that Sarah had enjoyed the snow and that she still did. She was angry with the horseman for spoiling her afternoon's excursion and angry with herself for not thinking ahead to avoid such a predicament. Knowing that she was in the wrong, she accepted liability and arrogantly promised to pay for any damage.

[Did you notice that the words quoted from the passage are in double inverted commas on the paper? You should do the same. This kind of thing varies from board to board, so be alert.]

At the end make sure that you have numbered your answers to match the questions; answered each part of a question; ruled out your rough work; and ruled off your completed work.

I hope you remembered to be brief but to give enough substance to each answer to earn the marks. Whatever you do, avoid rambling on without any sense of purpose and direction. The result will be waffle which scores absolutely nothing.

In the tests that follow, work on your own, timing yourself carefully. When you have completed a comprehension, check your answers against mine. Resist the temptation to look at the answers before you have done the work. That is not the best way to learn. Learn by doing and learn from your mistakes. That way your learning will be thorough.

Example 2

Example 2 is the completion of the paper started in the summary section – the one in which you had to summarize the advantages of employing police officers on foot-patrol (p. 67). So far, you have done half the first question. There are two questions on the paper. The rubric states:

'This paper tests your ability to read with understanding and to think about what you have read. Do not hurry. You have two fairly long passages in front of you, but enough time for reading them. You will be wise to get to know each passage well before attempting to answer any of the questions set on it.

Remember that this is an examination in English Language. It is important not only to answer the questions correctly but also to write your answers in clear, careful English, with proper attention to spelling and punctuation.'

See if you can finish the rest of question 1 (see p. 68) in 20 minutes.

1. [Did you remember to use inverted commas for 'foot-patrol officer'? This time you can use single or double, but be consistent throughout the paper.]
  (a) (i) A 'foot-patrol officer' is a police officer who walks the beat.
     (ii) The author thinks a foot-patrol officer should carry a walkie-talkie.
  (b) [Notice that you are to give the meanings of *three* words only in this question.]
     (i) 'flexible' means adaptable, suggesting a police force able to adapt to change.
     (ii) 'excessively' in this sense means noticeably: policemen merge into the darkness and are unobtrusive at night.
     (iii) a 'deterrent' is a restraint. The sight of a police officer is a restraining influence in the prevention of crime.
     (iv) 'vulnerable' means open to attack. The police officer on patrol duty is at risk.
  (c) You have already done this in the Summary Section.
  (d) To establish cordial public relations, the most suitable areas for the foot-patrols would be densely populated city suburbs with houses, shops and flats. The least suitable would be industrial estates, and districts from which the residents commute each day (39 words). [Did you remember to state the number of words?]

  2. Read carefully the following passage, and answer the questions set on it. Allow 1 hour.

Just short of the churchyard gates the shops discreetly ended, giving place to a group of more impressive houses, Georgian in date, their pillared doorways decorated by the brass plates of auctioneers, solicitors and joint-stock banks. In front of the small-est of these, a squat building faced with stucco, joined to one   5
neighbour, but separated from the other by a narrow passage, a red

lamp burned dimly, revealing in letters of uncoloured glass the word: SURGERY. A brass plate, so sedulously polished in bygone years that the sunken letters were almost flush with the surface, but now dull and tarnished, announced the name and qualifications of its owner: *John Hammond, L.S.A., L.R.C.S., Physician and Surgeon*. As he dumped his bag beside the worn sandstone steps, Jonathan was thinking how well *J. Dakers, M.B., M.Ch.* would look by the side of it. He had ordered the new plate in North Bromwich that morning.

He seized the brass bell-pull; an old-fashioned spring-bell echoed within. He waited. Along a flagged passage he heard a shuffle of slow feet. Whoever their owner might be, he was in no hurry. In a doctor's house, he thought, the bell should be answered more promptly. Then the door opened, and a young woman stared at him.

'Good evening,' he said. 'I think you're expecting me.'

'You are Dr. Dakers?' she answered. 'Step in, please.'

In the Black Country you are always told to step in.

'I'm sorry,' she went on. 'I'm afraid my father is out—at a midwifery case; he's been at it most of the day.'

'Then you are Miss Hammond?' Jonathan asked.

She nodded. 'You have your bag there? Please let me take it. I'd better show you to your room.'

She grasped the handle of the bag. As Jonathan forestalled her, his hand met hers.

'Nonsense!' he said. 'Whatever are you talking about? Of course I'll carry it myself, if you'll show me the way.'

She surrendered the bag without another word. He had the impression that her offer had been mechanical, the automatic gesture of a mind that was used to effacing itself, of hands that were accustomed to relieve hands older and feebler of all exertion.

'If you'll wait a second,' she said, 'I'll get some matches, so that we can light the gas upstairs.'

Before he had time to tell her he had a box in his pocket, she was gone. When she returned a moment later, the suspended gas light revealed her as a tall, dark young woman, probably of his own age. She wore a black skirt covered by a print apron, a black blouse, high at the neck, with a white frill and jabot, and the low-heeled leather slippers which Jonathan had heard dragging over the hall floor. Her body was big and powerful—he could see, at a glance,

that she could easily have carried his bag if he had let her—yet, for all its apparent strength, not without grace. Her face, indeed, had a certain solemn beauty: black hair, not dead, but with the life of copper in it, was swept back, like a Spaniard's, on either side   50
of an ivory parting; beneath it he saw a brow made serious by two horizontal furrows; black eyebrows, too heavy for beauty, whose straightness gave the dark eyes beneath them a look of slightly puzzled determination, as though their owner were used to fighting against odds; a straight, well-chiselled nose; lips, full and possibly   55
sulky, modified by the firmness of a mouth that was larger than it might have been and seemed redder for the healthy pallor of her face.

   She was, in fact, the complete physical opposite of the type that had always attracted Jonathan; yet even his prejudices could not   60
deny her a certain nobility. Without being in the least enchanted, he was impressed. Her black eyes met his unflinchingly; the full lips did not smile. He had the feeling that though nothing came from within her to meet him, some secret, inward tribunal was summing him up. Her scrutiny, though brief, was embarrassing.   65
He tried, in self-defence, to break it with a smile.

   'When I came here before,' he said. 'I didn't have the pleasure of seeing you.'

   It struck him that in some subtle way she would consider 'pleasure' to be the wrong word.   70

   'I was busy, both times,' she said. 'All the same, I saw you. I saw you pass the window when you were going away.'

   This time he dared to joke: 'Well, did you think I'd do?'

   Again her eyes considered him; her lips, for one moment, parted in a faint smile; her teeth were fine and regular, and very white   75
against the red lips. The dark straight brows contracted slightly; her voice was low, and dark like all the rest of her.

   'Yes,' she said, almost contemptuously. 'I suppose you'll do. You've got to do now, anyway, haven't you? Will you please step upstairs.'   80

   (FRANCIS BRETT YOUNG, *My Brother Jonathan*)

(*a*) Dr. Hammond's house is situated in a town which the author
      calls Wednesford. In what part of England is it?   [3]

(*b*) (i) What do you gather is to be the relationship between John
      Hammond and Jonathan Dakers?   [6]

   ii) In lines 67–72 there is a reference to two previous calls that Jonathan has made on John Hammond. What do you suppose was the purpose of those visits?

(c) *A brass plate, so sedulously polished* (line 8). Explain *sedulously*. [3]

(d) (i) *a flagged passage* (line 17). What do you understand by *flagged*? [9]

   (ii) *he heard a shuffle of slow feet* (lines 17–18). What caused the feet to *shuffle*?

   (iii) *In a doctor's house, he thought, the bell should be answered more promptly* (lines 19–20). Why should it?

(e) In lines 28–33 Miss Hammond tries to take Jonathan's suitcase from him and carry it upstairs. What does Jonathan deduce from this? (Answer in your own words as far as possible.) [3]

(f) Very briefly say what you understand by the italicized words: [9]

   (i) a straight, *well-chiselled* nose (line 55);

   (ii) even his *prejudices* (line 60);

   (iii) almost *contemptuously* (line 78).

(g) *It struck him that in some subtle way she would consider 'pleasure' to be the wrong word* (lines 69–70). What was it about Miss Hammond, do you think, that gave Jonathan this impression? [3]

(h) The action described in this passage took place some seventy years ago. Find in the passage, and write down, two pieces of evidence that suggest such a distance back in time. [4]

(i) Suppose that later that same evening Jonathan Dakers writes to his brother Harold. In one part of the letter he gives his first impressions of Miss Hammond, conveying something of her looks, her dress, and the kind of person she is, judging from this first encounter with her. In a paragraph of some 15–20 lines (120–150 words) write what you think might be that part of his letter. [20]

(Oxford Local Examinations, November 1982: 1801/2)

Here are the answers to question 2.

2. (a) Wednesford is in the Black Country, and so in that part of England where a caller is invited to 'step in'.

    (b) (i) John Hammond, a well-qualified and experienced physician and surgeon, has appointed the young and newly qualified Dr Jonathan Dakers as his junior partner.

    (ii) It seems likely that the young doctor had called once to attend an interview and once to finalize the arrangements for his new appointment.

    (c) 'sedulously': The brass plate had been polished with persistent attention until the surface brass had been worn down, and the engraved letters were almost on a level with it.

    (d) (i) 'flagged': The hall had a stone floor and the sound of feet being dragged along such a surface would be easily audible.

    (ii) 'shuffle': Sliding her leather slippers across the stone floor without picking her feet up, Miss Hammond caused her feet to 'shuffle'.

    (iii) A doctor can never know how urgent the needs of his caller will be until he has answered the door. This should be done with the least possible delay in case he has an emergency on his doorstep.

    (e) Jonathan deduces that Miss Hammond was used to waiting on others, especially her father, and that she regarded herself as unimportant.

    (f) (i) A 'well-chiselled nose' is a clear-cut, well-shaped nose and it was one of Miss Hammond's attractive features.

    (ii) 'prejudices': These are biassed opinions against that sort of woman, but even these could not prevent Jonathan from acknowledging Miss Hammond's bearing and elegance.

    (iii) 'contemptuously': Miss Hammond said, 'I suppose you'll do' in a scornful tone which suggested a complete lack of interest in the new doctor.

    (g) Jonathan had the impression that Miss Hammond would consider 'pleasure' the wrong word to use, because neither her severe appearance, nor her unfriendly manner suggested that pleasure was part of her experience.

    (h) The brass bell-pull that activated the spring-bell within was a relic of former times; so, too, was the gas lighting.

If you found some of those questions difficult, the last question gives you a generous opportunity to score well. It is based on direct understanding of the passage and, therefore, all the information is printed on the page in front of you. Remember that you are Jonathan writing to your brother, Harold, seventy years ago. Choose an appropriate register.

> (i) The doctor's daughter let me in and showed me to my room. I will not say she welcomed me – she was too cold – but she did offer to carry my bag, which struck me as strange. I had the impression that she waits on her father and that she finds life dreary these days. Anyone less like the kind of girl I admire would be hard to imagine. She is not without grace, but her face bears signs of strain. She is about my age. Her dark hair and eyes and lashes contrast with her pale complexion and red lips; her features are well-pronounced. She wears sombre black clothes; the white relief at the neck and throat did little to take away the severity. I recognize in her a woman of quiet dignity but I did not warm to her nor she to me ...
>
> (144 words)

The instructions were to write 'a paragraph of some 15–20 lines (120–150 words)' and it had to be *part* of a letter. There was no need for the letter form.

Now we shall look in detail at these answers to Example 2, question 2:

(a) As three marks are available, it is advisable to support your answer with relevant detail.

(b) 'What do you gather' means that you have to deduce the answer as it is not directly stated. You know that John Hammond is a qualified physician and surgeon, and because the brass plate that bears his name is well-worn, you can assume that he has been in practice for a long time. The other doctor, Jonathan Dakers, is probably newly qualified as he has just ordered his brass plate to put beside Dr Hammond's. This suggests that they are to be partners. There are three marks for the answer, so include enough substance to score three.

(c) This question asked for an explanation of the word, so it would not have been enough to answer in a word or phrase. You must explain the word as used in the passage. The same applies in (d) (i) and (ii).

(d) Notice the 9 marks and give enough information but do not waffle.

(f) Notice the instructions 'very briefly', but notice, too, that there are 9 marks. You must give sufficient detail, to score these marks. You must also be concise.

Example 3

2. Read the following passage carefully and then answer the questions on it.   (20 marks)

For me, exploration was a personal venture. I did not go to the Arabian desert to collect plants nor to make a map; such things were incidental. At heart I knew that to write or even to talk of my travels was to tarnish the achievement. I went there to find peace in the hardship of desert travel and the company of desert peoples.   5
I set myself a goal on these journeys, and although the goal itself was unimportant, its attainment had to be worth every effort and sacrifice. Scott had gone to the South Pole in order to stand for a few minutes on one particular and almost inaccessible spot on the Earth's surface. He and his companions died on their way back,   10
but even as they were dying he never doubted that the journey had been worth while. Everyone knew that there was nothing to be found on the top of Everest, but even in this materialistic age few people asked, "What point is there in climbing Everest? What good will it do everyone when they get there?" They recognised that   15
even today there are experiences that do not need to be justified in terms of material profit.

No, it is not the goal but the way there that matters, and the harder the way the more worth while the journey. Who, after all, would dispute that it is more satisfying to climb to the top of a   20
mountain than to go there in a funicular railway? Perhaps this was one reason why I resented modern inventions; they made the road too easy. I felt instinctively that it was better to fail on Everest without oxygen than to attain the summit with its use. If climbers used oxygen, why should they not have their supplies dropped to   25
them from aeroplanes, or landed by helicopter? Yet to refuse mechanical aids as unsporting reduced exploration to the level of a sport, like big-game shooting in Kenya when the hunter is allowed to drive up to within sight of the animal but must get out of the car to shoot it. I would not myself have wished to cross the   30
Arabian desert in a car. Luckily this was impossible when I did my journeys, for to have done the journey on a camel when I could have done it in a car would have turned the venture into a stunt.

WILFRED THESIGER

(a) What personal reason does the author give for his exploring the Arabian desert? (2 marks)

(b) What requirements did the goal have to satisfy in order to be acceptable to the author? (*Use your own words in your answer.*) (2 marks)

(c) To the author, what similarities are there between Scott's expedition and the ascent of Everest? (4 marks)

(d) Referring to the examples in the passage, explain how the worth and satisfaction of the various adventurous pursuits may be reduced. (4 marks)

(e) Explain *in your own words* the meaning of two of the following expressions as they are used in the passage. (4 marks)
  (i) this materialistic age (line 13)
  (ii) reduced exploration to the level of a sport (lines 27–28)
  (iii) turned the venture into a stunt (line 33)

(f) Choose four of the following words. For each give a word or short phrase which could be used to replace it in the passage without change of meaning.

incidental (line 3)	justified (line 16)
tarnish (line 4)	dispute (line 20)
inaccessible (line 9)	resented (line 22)

(4 marks)

(Associated Examining Board, June 1979: 025/2)

2. (a) The author explored the Arabian desert to test his powers of endurance under arduous conditions, to enjoy the fellowship of simple desert folk and to seek peace.

(b) The goal had to be worthy enough to justify the personal struggle and self-denial involved in attaining it.

(c) Scott had journeyed to the South Pole under conditions of extreme hardship that required courage of the highest order. The mountaineers who battled up the forbidding face of Everest stretched their physical powers to the limit and beyond. Both were seeking the satisfaction of achievement against impossible odds, and the spiritual fulfilment that this struggle gives.

(d) There is no merit in reaching the top of a mountain by funicular railway, but there are also less obvious ways of lessening the achievement. If a climber cannot reach the peak without oxygen, it would be better if he gave up at the point where he was physically exhausted. Anything that takes away the physical strain of man's struggle against the natural elements is to be deplored.

Much of the danger has been eliminated from big-game hunting. Nowadays the hunter travels by car in pursuit of his prey, and, although he has to get out of his vehicle to shoot, the level of the achievement has been reduced.

(e) [Note that only *two* are required.]

   (i) 'this materialistic age': This acquisitive period when people measure success in terms of possessions, having lost sight of the spiritual nature of existence.

   (ii) 'reduced exploration to the level of a sport': Expeditions requiring fortitude and courage have been put on a par with physical and pleasure-seeking activities.

   (iii) 'turned the venture into a stunt': Changed the nature of the exploration so that it became a cheap attention-seeking performance.

(f) [Note: choose *four*. As the words are not numbered on the question paper, you must write your *four* down one under the other as follows:]

incidental:	of minor significance
tarnish:	taint
inaccessible:	unreachable
justified:	excused
dispute:	argue
resented:	felt bitter about

[Test your words in the passage. Do they fit in comfortably without changing the meaning? They must match. For example, you cannot say 'feel bitter about' for 'resented'. It *must* be 'felt'.]

After this examination, the examiners said:

'The principal failings here were of three kinds: firstly, the failure to read the text carefully enough to understand it fully; secondly, the failure to refer to all the relevant parts of the text when compiling answers to the questions; and lastly, the failure to answer in concise, grammatical English.'

Example 4

2. Read the following passage carefully and then answer the questions on it.   (20 marks)

Having to write a preface after labouring for five years to produce a book is an unnerving experience and something of an anti-climax; rather like an elephant who has succeeded at long last in giving birth to her calf being then required to balance a bun on her head.   5

But a preface has its uses. It can give readers a whiff of the author's style and an indication of his potential as an inducer of tedium, thus enabling them to moderate their enthusiasm, lower their sights, and so prepare themselves for the main body of the work. A preface can also give the author a few precious moments   10 alone with a person who has bought the book, or is having a free read of it in a bookshop, or has borrowed it from a library by mistake, in which the author can explain what the book is about.

There have been many descriptions of what history is, but there are probably as many ways of looking at the past as there are writers   15 and historians prepared to look. This book is an attempt to look at social history from the viewpoint of people who were alive at the time and were not at all happy about what was going on.

As in most histories, my book is concerned with great personages and great deeds but the concern is with their imperfections, not   20 their glories; with the aspects of them which caused contemporaries to treat them with scorn, fury or ridicule. The approach is that of the judge who before considering sentence asks, "Is anything known against?" Thus the Wordsworth in this book is not the great nature poet but the Wordsworth with clammy hands and no sense   25 of smell; Rousseau is not the philosopher who tried to reform education but Rousseau the despiser of intelligent women. Embedded in the text are more than a thousand expressions of human displeasure, culled from poems, prose writings, letters, critical commentaries and reported speech. These range in power from   30 mild disapproval to blind hate.

In no sense is this book offered as a work of scholarship—the author would not make so bold—but as a highly personal account of social history seen from a rather unusual point of view. It is hoped that when this account is added to the more orthodox view of   35 history, the reader will end up with a slightly more stereoscopic picture of the past. Each chapter cannot possibly tell the whole story of course, so the aim has been to be representative rather than exhaustive.

FRANK MUIR

(a) Explain in your own words the author's feelings about having to write a preface to his book. (3 marks)

(b) According to the author, what does the reader gain from the preface? Use your own words. (4 marks)

(c) What purpose does a preface serve as far as the author is concerned? (2 marks)

(d) In what respect does Muir's book differ from most histories? (3 marks)

(e) Explain in your own words the meaning of the following:
 (i) "from mild disapproval to blind hate" (lines 30–31)
 (ii) "to be representative rather than exhaustive" (lines 38–39). (4 marks)

(f) Choose four of the following words. For each one give a word or short phrase that could replace it in the passage without changing the meaning.

    required (line 4)   culled (line 29)
    approach (line 22)   scholarship (line 32)
    embedded (lines 27–28)   orthodox (line 35)

                                         (4 marks)

(Associated Examining Board, June 1980: 025/2)

2. (a) After all his hard work and involvement over a long period creating his book, the author was disconcerted by having to write an introduction, regarding it as a descent from the inspired to the ridiculous.

(b) A reader gains a brief introduction to a writer's way of expressing himself, and can size up his chances of being bored. With the benefit of this fore-knowledge, he can then read the book adjusting his expectations and interest accordingly.

(c) The author is able to tell his readers what his book is about.

(d) Muir has written an unconventional history concentrating on the short-comings and failures of famous people which provoked feelings of disapproval at the time. Most histories are conventional accounts that record deeds of honour and great achievements.

(e) (i) 'from mild disapproval to blind hate': By using this phrase, Muir has included all the degrees of feeling from slight annoyance to senseless loathing.

    (ii) 'to be representative rather than exhaustive': To give typical examples of each period without attempting to present a comprehensive study.

(f) [N.B. Only *four* to be answered.]

Do remember to give words that can be substituted without altering the meaning.

required:	asked
approach:	method
embedded:	fixed firmly
culled:	selected
scholarship:	academic achievement
orthodox:	traditional

After this examination, the examiners said:

'As always, it was necessary for the questions to be read carefully before an answer was framed and written ...'

You know how important it is, so you will not throw away marks by failing to read the questions carefully. Many hundreds of candidates lost marks on this paper for careless misreading of the questions and for ignoring instructions, especially when told to 'use your own words'.

To save you from losing marks unnecessarily and to encourage you to produce work of the highest standard, I have suggested that you always use your own words. It is a good habit to cultivate.

Question (b) was misread by many hundreds. Instead of answering 'what does the reader gain ...' they quoted the author's gains. This carelessness and more besides during the course of the examination resulted in several marks being lost. Final results were often a grade lower than they need have been.

Multiple-choice Comprehension Test Examples

Our next three examples are multiple-choice tests. Read every text with the same care and attention as before. The main advantage now is that you are free to read and think without the worry of having to compose answers in your own words.

In the examples that follow, you have to select the correct answer from a choice of five. Some boards offer you a choice of four. It makes little difference. There is only one correct answer each time.

The objective-test booklet – so called because the examination is marked impersonally by a machine – arrives in the examination room complete with answer sheet. You are told to complete it and exactly what to do. If you are in any doubt at all, one of the invigilators (teachers in charge of the examination) will explain anything to you before the examination begins.

In the booklet you will find a passage, or passages, and questions, each with four or five possible answers. Only one answer is correct. The other answers are called 'distractors'. Do not let them distract you. The method is exactly the same as before. Concentrate, read and re-read until you understand.

As your work is marked by a computer, you have to make a clear black mark on the answer sheet, using a pencil, but in our practices just write down a letter answer: A, B, C, D or E.

Try this one and see if you can complete it in 15 minutes. Do not look at the answers until your time is up. Then work through the test with me. Refer to the corresponding question in the examination paper as you study each answer.

Example 5

COMPREHENSION PASSAGE 1

Questions 1 to **15** are based on this passage. Read the passage carefully; then answer the questions.

September is the month of memories. Perhaps this is due to the smell of autumn, half acrid like tanned leather, half of 'mellow fruitfulness', the ghosts of roses and apples on the shelves. And smells are the great conjurors of memories. A whiff of honeysuckle brings back to me, instantly, the garden of my childhood, with the　5
mother of the family standing, water-can in hand, talking to me across a thicket of Michaelmas daisies, with a veil of gnats, playing between us, and the sun flashing on her gold-rimmed spectacles. It is a poignant scene, saved from sadness by being so sacred. All that from a sprig of honeysuckle: the annihilation of over half a century.　10
Or perhaps the right word is not annihilation but distillation; for this process leaves an attar* of time, a tiny phial to be stored in the mind, whence it impregnates the personal universe.

---

* A fragrant oil distilled from roses.

I have just returned from a morning's outing with a grand-daughter who is developing, at an early age, a passion for domestic economy. She insisted, at the open door of my workroom where I had just begun to settle down to the habitual daily output of words, that I should take her out to gather blackberries, because she wanted Cook to teach her how to make bramble jelly. As I have a weakness for this conserve, I was not reluctant to leave pen and paper and submit myself to this diminutive tyrant.

We set off solemnly, with a mother and the grandmother to watch us go down the narrow lane between the honeysuckle hedges. Before we had lost sight of the watchers at the gate, the dachshund came rushing after us, whimpering with reproach at having been forgotten. He hurled himself along and pulled up gradually in front of us, to open at once into a scheme of investigation, criss-crossing the land from one hedge to the other with a nervous frequency that must have tested his brakes to the utmost.

At the bottom of the hill we stopped by the dell. We began to pick, but the best berries were too high. I lifted up my grand-daughter, seating her on my shoulders in the manner of a 'flying angel'. From that height she had approach to unlimited hoards of fruit. Cries of exultation came from above my head, and I felt a small pair of legs kick out with excitement, so that I almost stumbled into one of the clumps of bramble and deposited my burden into the middle of it.

Unable to help in the gathering, I furtively picked a vintage berry here and there and popped it into my mouth. At once the taste of childhood came back to me, and I stood there, a beast of burden, but now only about twelve years old, somewhere in the wilds of Hampshire, with my parents and elder brother on the other side of the bush, dressed in out-of-date clothes, exchanging conversation with me. I could hear the loved voices of those vanished dear ones; long since vanished.

1. Smells are called the 'great conjurors' of memories (line 4) because they

   A   change them into something else

   B   surprise us with unfamiliar experiences

   C   call them apparently from nowhere

   D   make them seem like ghosts

   E   deceive us by subtle tricks

2. The 'poignant scene' is 'saved from sadness' (line 9) because it is

   A   recreated by the smell of honeysuckle

   B   associated with memories which he treasures

   C   connected vaguely with his religious beliefs

   D   linked with the feast of Michaelmas

   E   recalled from the very distant past

3. The process, set in motion by the honeysuckle, is called 'distillation' (line 11) because it

   A   derives from the scent of the flowers

   B   silences everything for half a century

   C   lingers unchanged in the author's mind

   D   reduces fifty years to their essence

   E   brings back things with fragrant memories

4. Which one of the following words is closest in meaning to 'impregnates' as used in line 13?

   A   Dominates

   B   Pervades

   C   Conceives

   D   Shapes

   E   Disturbs

5. The first paragraph (lines 1–13) is mainly about

    A gardens which he remembers

    B memories which make him sad

    C events which recall his family

    D smells which evoke memories

    E months which are memorable

6. The author was 'not reluctant to leave pen and paper' (lines 20–21) because he was

    A fond of bramble jelly

    B too weak to decline

    C unable to settle down

    D very fond of the child

    E submissive to tyranny

7. Paragraph two (lines 14–21) suggests that the author is

    A irritable

    B timid

    C indulgent

    D lazy

    E insensitive

8. 'We set off solemnly' (line 22) most probably because

    A the man realized his responsibility

    B it was a serious matter for the child

    C the author resented the interruption

    D they wanted to avoid the frisky dog

    E the others were sorry to see them go

9. The 'scheme of investigation' (lines 27–28) was that the dachshund intended to

    A explore both sides of the lane

    B join the search for blackberries

    C discover why he had been left behind

    D make sure of the two people

    E test his powers of braking

10. The movements of the dachshund (lines 25–29) were characterized by all the following EXCEPT

    A   inquisitiveness

    B   great speed

    C   fearfulness

    D   constant stopping

    E   purposefulness

11. Which one of the following words is closest in meaning to 'dell' as used in line 30?

    A   Stream

    B   Gate

    C   Hollow

    D   Footpath

    E   Wood

12. There were 'Cries of exultation' (line 34) mainly because the little girl was

    A   being carried shoulder-high

    B   terrified of being dropped

    C   kicking out with excitement

    D   full of high spirits

    E   seeing lots of blackberries

13. Which one of the following words is closest in meaning to 'furtively' as used in line 38?

    A   Frustratedly

    B   Stealthily

    C   Delicately

    D   Largely

    E   Haphazardly

14. A 'vintage' berry (lines 38–39) is one which is

    A   suitable for wine-making

    B   particularly fine in quality

    C   indicative of a good year

    D   especially old and glossy

    E   reminiscent of former fruit

15. Eating a blackberry (lines 38–39) reminds the author of all the following EXCEPT

    A   his parents and brother

    B   clothes of long ago

    C   days spent blackberrying

    D   carrying gathered fruit

    E   voices from the past

(University of London, June 1980: 160/2)

Here are a check-list and the answers:

1. Conjurors are seemingly able to produce things from nowhere. When 'smells' produce 'memories' from nowhere, they can be figuratively 'conjurors'. C

2. Because the author treasures the memories, they are 'saved from sadness'. He likes to remember what he treasures even though the remembrance is sharply painful to him. B

3. In distillation, the essence is extracted, so the answer is D. If you did not know this, you could work it out. The fragrance of the honeysuckle reminded him of his childhood. Distillation leaves a fragrant oil, the memory of which can be stored in the mind to penetrate the personal world. When the fragrance is smelt again, the association of ideas reminds the person, who has stored the fragrance, of other days and the same perfume, thus reducing fifty years to their essence. D

4. Pervades. B

5. Do read closely so that you find the exact answer. The paragraph is mainly about 'smells' which evoke (call up) memories. D

6. A.

7. The author was not irritable or timid or lazy or insensitive in lines 14–21 so he must have been indulgent. He was lenient in his affectionate relationship with his grand-daughter. Some would say he spoilt her. C

8. 'it was a serious matter for the child'. B

9. 'explore both sides of the lane'. A

10. The dog's movements were everything except fearful. C

11. A dell is a wooded hollow. C

12. 'seeing lots of blackberries'. E

13. 'stealthily' is nearest in meaning to 'furtively'. B

14. Do not jump to the conclusion that vintage and wine always go together. Think first. The grandfather is most likely to pick the best blackberries if he is about to eat them. 'Vintage' means representing the best in this context. B

15. There is no mention of 'carrying gathered fruit' in the extract. D

Example 6

COMPREHENSION PASSAGE 2

Questions 11 to 36 are based on this passage. [35 minutes.]

My first impression was that the stranger's eyes were of an un-
usually light blue. They met mine for several blank seconds,
vacant, unmistakably scared. Startled and innocently naughty,
they were the eyes of a schoolboy surprised in the act of breaking
one of the rules. Not that I had caught him, apparently, at anything   5
except his own thoughts: perhaps he imagined I could read them.
At any rate, he seemed not to have heard or seen me cross the
compartment from my corner to his own, for he started violently at
the sound of my voice; so violently indeed, that his nervous recoil
hit me like repercussion. Instinctively I took a pace backwards.   10
It was exactly as though we had collided with each other bodily
in the street. We were both confused, both ready to be apologetic.
Smiling, anxious to reassure him, I repeated my question:
'I wonder, sir, if you could let me have a match?'
Even now, he didn't answer at once. He appeared to be engaged   15
in some sort of rapid mental calculation, while his fingers,
nervously active, sketched a number of flurried gestures round his
waistcoat. For all they conveyed, he might equally have been going
to undress, to draw a revolver, or merely to make sure that I hadn't
stolen his money. Then the moment of agitation passed from his   20
gaze like a little cloud, leaving a clear blue sky. At last he had
understood what I wanted:
'Yes, yes. Er—certainly. Of course.'
As he spoke he touched his left temple delicately with his finger-
tips, coughed and suddenly smiled. His smile had great charm. It   25
disclosed the ugliest teeth I had ever seen. They were like broken
rocks.
'Certainly,' he repeated. 'With pleasure.'
Delicately, with finger and thumb, he fished in the waistcoat
pocket of his expensive-looking soft grey suit, and extracted a gold   30
spirit-lighter. His hands were white, small and beautifully mani-
cured.
I offered him my cigarettes.

'Er—thank you. Thank you.'

'After you, sir.'   35

'No, no. Please.'

The tiny flame of the lighter flickered between us, as perishable
as the atmosphere which our exaggerated politeness had created.
The merest breath would have extinguished the one, the least
incautious gesture or word would have destroyed the other. The   40
cigarettes were both lighted now. We sat back in our respective
places. The stranger was still doubtful of me. He was wondering
whether he hadn't gone too far, delivered himself to a bore or a
crook. His timid soul was eager to retire. I, on my side, had nothing
to read. I foresaw a journey of utter silence, lasting seven or eight   45
hours. I was determined to talk.

'Do you know the time we arrive at the frontier?'

Looking back on the conversation, this question does not seem to
me to have been particularly unusual. It is true that I had no
interest in the answer; I wanted merely to ask something which   50
might start us chatting, and which wasn't, at the same time, either
inquisitive or impertinent. Its effect on the stranger was remark-
able. I had certainly succeeded in arousing his interest. He gave me
a long, odd glance, and his features seemed to stiffen a little. It was
the glance of a card-player who guesses suddenly that his opponent   55
holds a very strong hand and he had better be careful. At length
he answered, speaking slowly and with caution:

'I'm afraid I couldn't tell you exactly. In about an hour's time, I
believe.'

His glance, now vacant for a moment, was clouded again. An   60
unpleasant thought seemed to tease him like a wasp; he moved his
head slightly to avoid it. Then he added, with surprising petulance:

'All these frontiers . . . such a horrible nuisance.'

I wasn't quite sure how to take this. The thought crossed my
mind that he was perhaps some kind of mild internationalist. I   65
ventured encouragingly:

'They ought to be done away with.'

'I quite agree with you. They ought, indeed.'

There was no mistaking his warmth. He had a large blunt fleshy
nose and a chin which seemed to have slipped sideways. It was like   70
a broken concertina. When he spoke, it jerked crooked in the most
curious fashion and a deep cleft dimple like a wound surprisingly
appeared in the side of it. Above his ripe red cheeks, his forehead

was sculpturally white, like marble. A fringe of dark grey hair lay across it, compact, thick and heavy. After a moment's examination, 75 I realized, with extreme interest, that he was wearing a wig.

'Particularly,' I followed up my success, 'all these red-tape formalities; the passport examination, and so forth.'

But no. This wasn't right. I saw at once from his expression that I'd somehow managed to strike a new disturbing note. We were 80 speaking similar but distinct languages. This time, however, the stranger's reaction was not mistrust. He asked, with a puzzling air of frankness and unconcealed curiosity:

'Have you ever had trouble here yourself?'

It wasn't so much the question which I found odd, as the tone in 85 which he asked it. I smiled to hide my mystification.

'Oh no. Quite the reverse. Often they don't bother to open anything; and as for your passport, they hardly look at it.'

'I'm so glad to hear you say that.'

He must have seen from my face what I was thinking, for he 90 added hastily: 'It may seem absurd of me, but I do so hate being fussed and bothered.'

'Of course. I quite understand.'

I grinned, for I had just arrived at a satisfactory explanation of his behaviour. The old boy was engaged in a little innocent private 95 smuggling. Probably a piece of silk for his wife or a box of cigars for a friend. And now, of course, he was beginning to feel scared. Certainly he looked prosperous enough to pay any amount of duty. The rich have strange pleasures.

Directions.

Questions 11 to 36 are based on **Passage 2**. Read the passage carefully and then answer the questions. Each question has five suggested answers. Select the best answer to each question.

11. Which *two* of the following
    are chiefly implied by the
    comparison of the stranger's
    eyes to those of 'a schoolboy
    surprised in the act of
    breaking one of the rules'
    (lines 4–5)? The stranger
    seemed to be

    1 disturbed by a simple
      request

    2 expecting a sudden
      blow

    3 caught out in some
      wrongdoing

    4 pretending to be
      innocent

    5 taken aback to find
      himself observed

    A   1 and 3 only

    B   1 and 4 only

    C   2 and 4 only

    D   2 and 5 only

    E   3 and 5 only

12. The author wondered,
    'perhaps he imagined I could
    read [his thoughts]' (line 6)
    probably because

    A   the stranger must have
        been about to commit
        some illegal act

    B   they had been looking
        very intently into each
        other's eyes

    C   the author's request
        seemed to show
        suspicion of the
        stranger

    D   there was no external
        reason for the sudden
        guilty reaction

    E   the stranger seemed
        ashamed of what he had
        in mind

13. 'Recoil' (line 9) indicates that
    the stranger

    A   jerked back abruptly

    B   withdrew into his
        thoughts

    C   tried to hide something

    D   prepared to defend
        himself

    E   shrank away timidly

14. The author's pace backwards (line 10) was essentially

   A   an apologetic movement

   B   a polite withdrawal

   C   a defensive gesture

   D   a response to danger

   E   an automatic reaction

15. The stranger's first reaction, when addressed by the author, was to

   A   look at him blankly

   B   make a sudden move

   C   pretend he was day-dreaming

   D   adopt an innocent attitude

   E   utter a nervous exclamation

16. In the first paragraph (lines 1–10) which *two* of the following seem to the author the likeliest reasons for the stranger's violent reaction? The stranger

   1   had been unaware of the author's approach

   2   was in fear of being physically attacked

   3   had thought he was alone in the compartment

   4   experienced some feeling of guilt in his mind

   A   1 and 3 only

   B   1 and 4 only

   C   2 and 3 only

   D   2 and 4 only

   E   3 and 4 only

17. The author was confused (line 12) primarily because he had

   A   been affected by physical shock

   B   not expected so violent a reaction

   C   anticipated no difficulty in getting a light

   D   not meant to start a conversation

   E   interrupted the stranger's private thoughts

18. Which two of the following are closest in meaning to 'flurried' as used in line 17?

    1 Agitated

    2 Jerky

    3 Vague

    4 Hasty

    5 Trembling

A 1 and 3 only

B 1 and 4 only

C 2 and 3 only

D 2 and 5 only

E 4 and 5 only

19. Which one of the following words is closest in meaning to 'conveyed' as used in line 18?

A Transferred

B Indicated

C Signalled

D Illustrated

E Achieved

20. The moment of agitation passed from the stranger's gaze (lines 20–21) because he

A found his mental calculations to be correct

B realized that he had not been robbed

C saw that he was not going to be attacked

D recognized the author as a former acquaintance

E perceived what it was that he was being asked

21. Which *three* of the following were responsible for the stranger's reactions as described in lines 1–22?

    1 Alarm

    2 Innocence

    3 Suspicion

    4 Incomprehension

    5 Anxiety

A 1, 2 and 3 only

B 1, 2 and 5 only

C 1, 4 and 5 only

D 2, 3 and 4 only

E 3, 4 and 5 only

22. The appearance of the stranger's hands seems to clash with that of his

    A   eyes

    B   suit

    C   smile

    D   lighter

    E   teeth

23. The comparison of the atmosphere between the two men to the flame of the lighter (lines 37–38) chiefly implies that their relationship was

    A   hostile

    B   over-polite

    C   precarious

    D   short-lived

    E   suspicious

24. The most probable reason for the politeness being exaggerated (line 38) was that both men

    A   wanted to conceal their thoughts and intentions for the time being

    B   intended to keep the relationship on a rather formal level

    C   hoped to impress each other with their good manners and behaviour

    D   wished to cover up the embarrassment caused by their first encounter

    E   came to realize that they had misjudged each other very badly

25. According to lines 49–52, the author, in asking his question about the frontier, had tried to avoid giving the appearance of

    A   prying into the stranger's private affairs

    B   arousing the stranger's nervous reaction

    C   being disrespectful to an older man

    D   sounding like a boring companion

    E   interrupting the stranger's peace and quiet

26. From the effect on the stranger of the question about the frontier (lines 52–56), it can be inferred that he

   A had no idea when they would arrive at the frontier

   B suspected that the question might conceal some threat to him

   C wanted to discuss whether there should be frontiers between countries

   D realized that the author was not familiar with the route

   E was unwilling to engage in any conversation with his companion

27. The stranger's glance (lines 53–56) suggested that he

   A realized the author was trying to start a conversation

   B was always suspicious of questions which seemed straightforward

   C believed the author knew more than the question revealed

   D tried to hide his true feelings from his fellow travellers

   E understood the author's reason for asking the question

28. The comparison of the stranger's thought to a wasp (lines 60–62) suggests all the following EXCEPT that the thought was

   A distracting his attention

   B a source of bother

   C difficult to ignore

   D a recurrent irritation

   E stinging him into speech

29. The word 'ventured' (line 66) implies that the author was

    A   uncertain what effect his remark might have

    B   pretending to share the stranger's point of view

    C   determined to find out more about the stranger

    D   attempting to arouse yet another interesting reaction

    E   unconcerned by the stranger's curious behaviour

30. The author's 'success' (line 77) was in

    A   perceiving why the stranger had behaved so oddly

    B   discovering roughly the time they would reach the frontier

    C   realizing that the stranger was wearing a wig

    D   having said the right thing to prolong the conversation

    E   persuading the stranger that frontiers should be abolished

31. The phrase 'red-tape formalities' (lines 77–78) is best explained as meaning unnecessarily

    A   restrictive international barriers

    B   strict police enquiries

    C   rigid official procedures

    D   complicated governmental rules

    E   severe customs duties

32. The sentence, 'We were speaking similar but distinct languages' (lines 80–81), implies that the two men were

    A   pretending to discuss certain matters but were interested in some other topic

    B   speaking dialects belonging to the same language but with different meanings

    C   agreeing with each other's opinions but really holding entirely opposed views

    D   talking about the same subjects but with quite different concerns in mind

    E   conversing with apparent ease but completely misunderstanding each other's meaning

33. The author 'smiled' (line 86) in order to hide the fact that he

    A   intended to discover the stranger's secret motives

    B   was pretending that frontier inspections were casual

    C   knew little about what happened at the frontier

    D   was puzzled by the stranger's odd reaction

    E   planned to conceal his own private affairs

34. The stranger displayed all of the following EXCEPT

    A   apprehension

    B   despair

    C   disquiet

    D   suspicion

    E   curiosity

35. In his dealings with the stranger, the author is at various times all of the following EXCEPT

    A   suddenly surprised

    B   pleasantly reassuring

    C   extremely polite

    D   tactfully encouraging

    E   cheerfully familiar

36. From the passage, all the following about the author can be inferred EXCEPT that he was

    A   fond of striking up conversations with strangers

    B   sensitive to the atmosphere in personal relationships

    C   aware of implications in other people's behaviour

    D   interested in understanding the motives of others

    E   eager to interfere in other people's business

(University of London, January 1982: 160/2)

Refer to the corresponding question in the examination paper as you study each answer.

11. The answer is E because a schoolboy 'caught out in some wrongdoing' would be 'taken aback to find himself observed'.　E
12. 'there was no external reason for the sudden guilty reaction'.　D
13. 'jerked back abruptly'.　A
14. We know it was 'an automatic reaction' because the word 'instinctively' suggests it.　E
15. The stranger 'started violently' so the answer must be B ('made a sudden move').　B
16. 1 and 4. It could not be 2 because the author had said nothing to suggest fear of attack, nor 3 because the stranger would be aware that he was not alone in the compartment.　B
17. The author was so surprised by the stranger's reaction that he was confused.　B
18. 'nervously active' is the clue to 'agitated' and 'a number of' suggests 'hasty' – a number of *hasty* gestures round his waist-coat.　B
19. 'indicated'.　B
20. Your close reading will have revealed that it cannot be the first four, so even if you do not know what 'perceived' means, you can make an intelligent guess that E is the correct answer.　E
21. You know that 'anxiety' was one, so the answer must have a 5 in it. B has a 5 in it – 'alarm' and 'innocence'? The stranger *was* alarmed, but he was not innocent. The word was used in the comparison to the schoolboy. That eliminates (or rules out) B. C has a 5 in it. Alarm? – yes. Incomprehension? – yes: 'at last he had understood' (lines 21–22) – so the previous incomprehension is indirectly stated here. Anxiety? – yes.　C
22. Look how his teeth are described in lines 26–27, and his hands in lines 31–32. That is a clash if ever there was one.　E
23. They were not 'hostile', or unfriendly. They *were* over-polite, but we know that; it does not have to be implied. 'Precarious'? Do you know what it means? Leave it for a moment. 'Short-lived'? Not really because it means lasting only a short time. It is true that the flame and the atmosphere may last only a short time and that

'the merest breath' or 'incautious gesture or word' could destroy each respectively; but there is an element of chance suggested in the text. It was fragile and insecure and therefore the right answer is 'precarious'.   C

24. D.

25. A.

26. The stranger gave the author 'a long, odd glance, and his features seemed to stiffen a little'. Why should he respond like that unless he 'suspected that the question might conceal some threat to him'?   B

27. Similarly 'he believed the author knew more than the question revealed'.   C

28. This is the kind of question that catches out the superficial readers. They see the word 'wasp' and immediately decide that 'stinging' must be part of the answer. It is, in fact, the odd one out, and so the answer is E.   E

29. We 'venture' something when the outcome is uncertain.   A

30. Having taken a chance and 'ventured' the author was pleased to note that the stranger responded warmly. Thus his 'success' was 'having said the right thing to prolong the conversation'.   D

31. Did you put C for this one? Correct if you did. The others are distractors.   C

32. You can eliminate all of these except D which is the correct answer.   D

33. Sometimes we smile to hide embarrassment, or something we have not understood as the author did here; 'mystification' in the text leads us to 'puzzled' in the answer. A, B, C and E have no connection with the text.   D

34. The stranger did not despair at any stage, but he was uneasy (apprehensive), worried (disquieted), suspicious and curious.   B

35. The author was never 'cheerfully familiar'.   E

36. The author was obviously A, B, C and D, but at no stage was he E.   E

Example 7

COMPREHENSION PASSAGE 3

Questions 42 to **60** are based on this passage. Read the passage carefully; then answer the questions [30 minutes].

Corfu lies off the Albanian and Greek coast-lines like a long, rust-eroded scimitar. The hilt of the scimitar is the mountain region of the island, for the most part barren and stony with towering rock cliffs haunted by blue-rock thrushes and peregrine falcons. In the valleys in this mountain region, however, where 5 water gushes plentifully from the red and gold rocks, you get forests of almond and walnut trees, casting shade as cool as a well, thick battalions of spear-like cypress and silver-trunked fig trees with leaves as large as a salver. The blade of the scimitar is made up of rolling greeny-silver eiderdowns of giant olives, some 10 reputedly over five hundred years old and each one unique in its hunched, arthritic shape, its trunk pitted with a hundred holes like pumice stone. Towards the tip of the blade you have Lefkimi with its twinkling, eye-aching sand dunes and great salt marshes, decorated with acres of bamboos that creak and rustle to each other 15 surreptitiously.

Summer gaped upon the island like the mouth of a great oven. Even in the shade of the olive groves it was not cool and the incessant penetrating cries of the crickets seemed to swell and become more insistent with each hot noon. The water in the ponds 20 and ditches shrank and the mud at the edges became jigsawed, cracked and curled by the sun. The sea lay as breathless and still as a length of silk, the shallow waters too warm to be refreshing. You had to row a boat out into deep water, you and your reflection the only moving things, and dive over the side to get cool. It was like 25 diving into the sky.

One little bay became a favourite haunt of mine, and nearly every afternoon, while the family were having their siesta, I would make my way down to it. It was so full of life that I scarcely knew where to begin my collecting. Under and on top of the rocks were 30 the chalky white tunnels of the tube worms, like some swirling and complicated pattern of icing sugar on a cake, and in the slightly deeper water there were stuck in the sand what appeared to be lengths of miniature hose pipe. If you stood and watched carefully,

a delicate, feathery, flowerlike cluster of tentacles would appear at   35
the ends of the hose pipes—tentacles of iridescent blue and red and
brown that would turn slowly round and round. These were the
bristle worms. Here and there on the sandy floor of the bay were
half-moons of black shiny ribbon-weed looking like dark feather
boas, anchored to the sand, and in these you would find pipe fish,   40
whose heads looked extraordinarily like elongated sea horses,
perched on the end of a long slender body.

It was in this bay that I caught my first spider crab. I would
have walked right past him thinking him to be a weed-covered
rock, if he had not made an incautious movement. His body was   45
about the size and shape of a small flattened pear and at the pointed
end it was decorated with a series of spikes, ending in two horn-
like protuberances over his eyes. His legs and his pincers were
long, slender and spindly. But the thing that intrigued me most was
the fact that he was wearing, on his back and on his legs, a complete   50
suit of tiny sea-weeds, which appeared to be growing out of his
shell. Enchanted by this weird creature, I carried him triumphantly along the beach to a rock pool and placed him in it. The firm
grip with which I had had to hold him had rubbed off much of his
sea-weed suit. I placed him in the shallow clear water and watched   55
to see what he would do. Standing high on his toes, like a spider
in a hurry, he scuttled a foot or so away from where I had put him
and then froze. He sat like this for a long time, so that I thought
he was going to remain immobile for the rest of the day, recovering
from the shock of capture, when he suddenly extended a long   60
delicate claw and daintily, almost shyly, plucked a tiny piece of sea-
weed which was growing on a nearby rock, and put it to his mouth.
At first I thought that he was eating it, but I soon realised I was
mistaken, for, with angular grace, he placed his claw over his back,
felt around in a fumbling way, and then planted the piece of weed   65
on his carapace. I presumed that he had been making the base of
the weed sticky to make it adhere to his back.

As I watched him he trundled slowly round the pool collecting a
variety of sea-weed with the assiduous dedication of a professional
botanist in a hitherto unexplored jungle. Within an hour his back   70
was covered with such a thick layer of growth that, if he sat still
and I took my eyes off him for a moment, I had difficulty in knowing exactly where he was.

Directions

Questions **42** to **60** are based on Passage 3. Read the passage carefully and then answer the questions. Each question has five suggested answers. Select the best answer to each question.

42. A 'scimitar' (line 2) is a

   A long rapier

   B curved sword

   C narrow scythe

   D thin dagger

   E pointed sickle

43. Which one of the following words is closest in meaning to 'barren' as used in line 3?

   A Rocky

   B Infertile

   C Uninhabited

   D Inhospitable

   E Dry

44. 'Cliffs haunted by blue-rock thrushes and peregrine falcons' (lines 4–5) is best explained as meaning that these birds

   A frighten other birds

   B look like ghosts

   C frequent that area

   D are rarely seen

   E fly about silently

45. Which *three* of the following are suggested by the reference to the cypresses as 'battalions' (line 8)? The trees are

   1 in close order

   2 fighting for survival

   3 great in number

   4 used for spears

   5 of similar appearance

   A 1, 2 and 3 only

   B 1, 2 and 4 only

   C 1, 3 and 5 only

   D 2, 4 and 5 only

   E 3, 4 and 5 only

46. Which one of the following is closest in meaning to 'salver' as used in line 9?

   A Wheel used on chariots

   B Coin made of silver

   C Tray used for presentations

   D Sword borne in procession

   E Shield used in battle

47. The statement that each of the olives is 'unique' (line 11) means that they are all

    A outstanding

    B different

    C separate

    D eccentric

    E uncommon

48. Which *two* of the following are suggested by the word 'arthritic' (line 12) when applied to the olives?

    1 Diseased

    2 Bent

    3 Twisted

    4 Broken

    5 Stunted

    A 1 and 3 only

    B 1 and 4 only

    C 2 and 3 only

    D 2 and 5 only

    E 4 and 5 only

49. Which one of the following best summarizes the main contents of the first paragraph (lines 1–16)?

    A The chief attraction of Corfu is its extraordinary scimitar shape. At one end of the long island are rugged mountains and fruitful valleys; in the middle, vast rolling plantations of bent and twisted olives cover the earth; and, at the other end, are expanses of sand dunes and marshes.

    B Everywhere in Corfu there is something worthy of attention. In the mountain valleys thick forests provide cool shade; among the olive groves, ancient trees bend and twist like crippled old men, while across the glittering sands and salt marshes near Lefkimi bamboos murmur mysteriously to each other.

    C Corfu is an island of extremely varied vegetation. In the valleys among the mountains there is ample water, and almond-trees, walnut trees, cypresses and fig-trees grow abundantly; at the other end of the island, bamboos grow among dunes and marshes. Between them lie rich plantations of olives.

    D Corfu is a scimitar-shaped island off

the Greek and Albanian coasts. At one end, are barren mountains with well-watered valleys wooded with nut-trees, cypresses and fig-trees; in the middle are large olive groves; and, at the other end, near Lefkimi, bamboos grow among sand dunes and salt marshes.

E   Corfu is a long, narrow country, near Albania and Greece, with mountains at one end, dunes and marshes at the other and, between them downs covered with olive-trees. It produces nuts, figs, olives and bamboo: its characteristic birds are blue-rock thrushes and peregrine falcons; its chief town is Lefkimi.

50. Which *two* of the following are implied by the word 'jig-sawed' as used in line 21? The mud was

1   divided and cross-divided by wandering cracks

2   broken into small bits and scattered

3   split into many separate irregular shapes

4   fretted and cracked by the water

A   1 and 2 only

B   1 and 3 only

C   2 and 3 only

D   2 and 4 only

E   3 and 4 only

51. Diving into the sea from a boat 'was like diving into the sky' (lines 25–26) because the

A   sea was as warm as the air above it

B   sky seemed much bluer than the sea

C   sea and the sky seemed to merge into one

D   sky was perfectly reflected in the calm water

E   sea was as attractive as paradise itself

52. 'One little bay became a favourite haunt' (line 27) of the writer mainly because

  A it enabled him to escape his family

  B of the solitude to be found there

  C of the richness of its natural life

  D of the unspoiled beauty of its setting

  E it passed the time during hot afternoons

53. The tunnels of the tube worms were like a 'pattern of icing sugar on a cake' (line 32) because of all the following EXCEPT their

  A shape

  B windings

  C hollowness

  D intricacies

  E colour

54. 'Feather boas' (lines 39–40) are

  A floating patches of very light seaweed

  B large snakes which crush their prey

  C curved headdresses of certain Indian tribes

  D decorative garments worn by ladies

  E tropical birds with dark glistening plumage

55. The author carried the crab 'triumphantly' (lines 52–53) probably because he was rejoicing in having

  A preserved the crab's disguise

  B discovered a new species

  C captured an extraordinary creature

  D found what he sought

  E evaded the crab's pincers

56. The comparison of the crab's behaviour to 'the assiduous dedication of a professional botanist' (lines 69–70) implies all of the following EXCEPT that he was

A   selecting his plants with great care

B   devoting himself single-mindedly to his task

C   carrying his collection on his back

D   working with diligence and persistence

E   making use of his skill and experience

57. The spider crab appears to be able to do all the following EXCEPT

A   merge completely into its background

B   live entirely on certain seaweeds

C   remain immobile for long periods

D   move quite rapidly when necessary

E   render things adhesive by chewing

58. The writer experienced all the following reactions to the spider crab EXCEPT

A   surprise at how it used seaweeds

B   fascination by its unusual appearance

C   excitement on succeeding in capturing it

D   concern about its continued survival

E   curiosity about the way it behaved

59. The style of the passage exhibits all the following EXCEPT

A   striking comparisons

B   impersonal manner

C   carefully observed details

D   enthusiastic tone

E   vivid descriptions

60. The passage reveals all the following about the writer EXCEPT that he is

   A patient in pursuing his studies

   B a collector of sea-shore creatures

   C especially interested in natural curiosities

   D a careful student of wild life

   E a scientist who earns his living from the sea-shore

STOP

Now go back and check your work.

(University of London, January 1981: 160/2)

Refer to the corresponding question in the examination paper as you study each answer.

42. If you do not know, you will have to guess. It is not easy to deduce from the text so ask yourself which is the most likely shape, bearing in mind the mountains, olive groves, sand dunes, salt marshes and sea.   B

43. You can deduce that stony ground is infertile ground, and that B is the correct answer; 'rocky' is too similar to stony and the other three make little sense.   B

44. There is nothing in the passage to suggest that birds 'look like ghosts' or that they 'frighten other birds'. D and E are incorrect. The answer is C.   C

45. A battalion of men is a large collection of soldiers in close order, dressed for battle. The reference suggests the cypresses were growing in close order, great in number and of similar appearance.   C

46 A 'salver' is a 'tray used for presentations' – it is usually silver.   C

47. If something is unique, there is only one of its kind, therefore all the olives were different.   B
48. 'Arthritic' here means bent and twisted.   C
49. This is difficult, but not impossible to work out. The first sentence of A is inaccurate, so we can eliminate that. In B the language is too figurative for a summary. C has left out Lefkimi. E sounds like a geography textbook and has omitted the well-watered valleys. D
50. The mud was 'divided and cross-divided by wandering cracks' and it was 'split into many separate irregular shapes'.   B
51. All the answers are ridiculous except D.   D
52. The author revelled in 'the richness of its natural life'.   C
53. There are no hollows on an iced cake, nor in the tunnels of the tube worms.   C
54. Feather boas were long scarves made of feathers or 'decorative garments worn by ladies'. Use your powers of deduction in a question like this. To say that 'half-moons of black shiny ribbon-weed looking like dark feather boas ...' could be A: 'floating patches of very light seaweed' is unimaginative; B: 'large snakes which crush their prey' is inappropriate; C: 'curved headdresses of certain Indian tribes' and E: 'tropical birds with dark glistening plumage' are both unlikely when you consider that they were 'anchored to the sand'.   D
55. He was triumphant because the creature was an extraordinary prize to have captured.   C
56. The crab did not carry his collection on his back but he did all the other things that botanists do. Did you guess that 'assiduous' means 'persevering'?   C
57. We are not told that the spider crab can live on seaweed, nor can we infer it from the account.   B
58. He did not think about its continued survival.   D
59. This is a very personal piece of well-observed writing, so 'impersonal manner' is the answer.   B
60. We cannot assume that the writer is 'a scientist who earns his living from the sea-shore', but we know without a doubt that A, B, C and D are true.   E

4 Composition

A composition is an original and complete piece of continuous writing arranged in paragraphs. It has a beginning, a middle and an end.

It trains you to express yourself in exact terms, to develop ideas of your own, to arrange your thoughts in an orderly fashion, and to communicate to different audiences. The examiners are looking to see if you have something interesting to say and whether you can say it effectively.

During your general reading, you have spent many hours studying other people's ideas, experiences, and opinions and reading their descriptions, narratives and reflections. Much of what you have read will have delighted you; some of it will have disturbed you; all of it will have set you thinking.

You have lived a variety of lives and shared a multitude of experiences vicariously – that is, you have lived and shared them at second hand, being absorbed in the writers' words. Those thoughts and feelings have now become part of your observation, enriching your life and fuelling your imagination. You can find the full range of emotional experience on the printed page.

'Reading maketh a full man . . .' said Francis Bacon; he added, 'and writing an exact man' ('Of Studies').

SKILLS TESTED

  (i) Your ability to make yourself easily understood in writing.
 (ii) Your ability to write interestingly and with relevance.
(iii) Your mastery of the basic skills described in Section 1.

(iv) Your ability to construct sentences that vary in length, rhythm and pattern.

(v) Your skill in giving each paragraph its own unity while, at the same time, relating each one to the following one, and to the overall unity of the composition – the development of a line of thought, narrative, argument or description.

(vi) Your ability to provide an arresting start and a satisfactory finish to your work.

(vii) Your ability to include some imagery and well–observed detail in your writing.

(viii) Your workmanship.

Let us look at these skills in close up:

(i) *Making yourself understood*: In general conversation you make yourself understood by using words naturally. When writing, do the same thing. If you have someone in mind, and imagine that you are speaking directly to that person, the words will come naturally. Form a complete sentence in your head before you begin to write it. Think about the sound and flow of the words. Listen to the rhythm.

Write the words as they flow; add a touch of formality at the revision stage. After a while, that revision stage will happen in your head and you will write clear and accurate English as a matter of course.

(ii) *Writing relevantly*: Writing relevantly is something that many candidates seem unable to do. The following advice is based on examiners' warnings after they had marked the compositions listed:

(a) A holiday I shall never forget.

(b) The advantages and disadvantages of shopping precincts in town centres.

(c) Write a descriptive account of a ceremony which has impressed you. You may choose one in which you took part or one where you were part of the audience.

(d) Entertaining friends.

(a) Do not spoil a composition of this type by writing irrelevant details of the holiday preparations. Direct your thinking on the holiday, decide why you will never forget it and write only about that.

(b) Do read the title carefully. This particular composition was misread and misunderstood by large numbers of candidates. They wrongly assumed that it was an invitation to weigh up the benefits or otherwise of shopping in supermarkets.

(c) If you are asked to describe 'a ceremony which has impressed you', that is what you must do. Wasting time writing about the irrelevant preparations is foolhardy. All your thinking should be focused on the ceremony.

(d) Similarly with this one. Long, tedious details about the preparations would be irrelevant, although a brief reference would be appropriate in this particular case. Concentrate on the social occasion.

Irrelevancy causes more failures in Composition – and consequently in the English Language Examination – than any other single mistake. You cannot score any marks for writing that has not been set, so that if, for example, your title is 'A holiday I shall never forget' and you take a page and a half to write about events and details connected with the preparations, that will be a page and a half that scores nothing. It sounds hard; it is hard. Judge relevance wisely. Bear the title in mind throughout your writing and keep to the point.

(iii) *Basic skills* (see Section 1): Persevere if you are still having problems.

(iv) *Sentences*: Have you noticed anything else about sentences in addition to the points mentioned on pp. 33–9? Have you been aware that constructions vary or that patterns change? Sometimes the main thought comes at the beginning, sometimes at the end and sometimes in the middle of a sentence.

There are other variations which you should look out for, too. The length of your sentences will determine the pace of your writing. Short sentences suggest urgency and speed: longer sentences a quieter pace. If you vary the length and pace to match your meaning, you will add life to your work and hold your readers' interest. You can make melody with words and put rhythm into your continuous writing.

Show the examiners that you know several ways of joining ideas. Use '-ing' words; 'who', 'whom', 'whose', 'which' and 'that'; other joining words in addition to 'and', 'but' and 'so' – you will find a list on p. 13. If you are not sure how to use any of these, you will find many examples in your general reading.

(v) *Paragraphs*: A paragraph is to a composition what a chapter is to a book; it is a collection of carefully constructed sentences that develops the idea stated in the key sentence. (For the O-level examination, never write a one-sentence paragraph.) Each paragraph deals with a particular aspect of the main subject; it is a self-contained unit, but, at the same time, a vital part of the whole to which it relates. A paragraph has a definite shape, pattern and rhythm.

Create your paragraphs with the eye of an artist and the ear of a musician, and you will be assured of a satisfying experience. Simplicity must be your keynote. No language is simpler than the perfect language of the New Testament, and many writers have found their inspiration there.

Strike a happy medium in the length of your paragraphs. If they are too short, your work will be disjointed; if they are too long, it will be tedious. Your paragraph is your vehicle for unfolding your line of thought, or expanding your description, or developing your argument, or relating your narrative. Polished paragraphs are the stuff that success is made of. Persevere.

Make links wherever possible, following the examples that you can find on the printed page. You will learn far more by analysing how writers move from one paragraph to the next than by trying to understand by reading about it.

As a general guide look out for:

(a) A brief reference in one paragraph that is developed in the next.
(b) A different aspect of the same subject introduced by words like 'another', 'in addition', 'similarly', 'yet'.
(c) A complete contrast introduced by words like 'on the other hand', 'however', 'nevertheless', 'consider', 'in contrast'.
(d) The introduction of a new subject which has no obvious connection with the preceding paragraph, but which is related to the title and therefore has an implied link. Sometimes the word 'secondly' can be used provided that 'first' was used earlier. If you pay attention to paragraph construction, your finished work will be a credit to you.

(vi) *Beginnings and endings*: It is absurd to begin a composition with a dreary account of waking up on a sunny/foggy/rainy summer/winter morning; washing, dressing, eating, loading the car and going on a journey. Plunge straight in. Never lose sight of the fact that your script is one of several hundred that an examiner has to mark. You must catch his attention and arouse his interest with your very first sentence.

Start with:

An unusual or unexpected remark.
A question.
A strange but relevant fact.
A quotation.
A witty comment if humour comes easily to you.
Any original sentence.

If you are one of the few who are able to write a story, your first sentence must be compelling otherwise your readers will not be keen to read on.

Right from the beginning, be lively and enthusiastic. Your first paragraph should be a tasty starter that whets the appetite for the main course.

The final paragraph should round off your work with an appropriate conclusion. Again, do not state the obvious with words like 'In conclusion I would like to say that . . .' nor repeat what you have already said as a summary. Try instead to be thought-provoking, or to leave your readers with a smile. Can you tell a brief anecdote that has a direct bearing on the subject matter, or look to the past or the future to make a comparison, or introduce an unexpected thought, or link your last sentence to your first?

Whatever you do, *do not wake up at the end and discover that it had all been a dream*!

(vii) *Imagery and well-observed detail*: The pictures that we conjure up in our imaginations are called images, and these used in writing make the work graphic so that it appeals to the senses. We talk about the 'imagery' of a piece of writing, meaning that the writer has made us see and feel what is being described. Would you be surprised to know that it is not the 'describing' words nor the '-ly' words that make these pictures – although they have a significant part to play? It is the 'naming' words and 'doing' words (nouns and verbs) that are the most vivid.

People, places, animals and things (nouns) can readily be received by the senses so that an image forms in the mind's eye. The same is true of the actions performed. For example:

Waves pounded the *rocks.*
Fireworks exploded in the *sky.*
Raindrops trickled down the *window pane.*

are clear images. Add 'describing' words and '-ly' words and the pictures become sharper:

Giant waves pounded the rocks *relentlessly.*
Brilliant fireworks exploded *spectacularly* in the *dark* sky.
Translucent raindrops trickled *sadly* down the window pane.

Choose your words with care. Avoid vague words like 'someone', 'it', 'this', 'people', and similar words that do not produce immediate pictures. Obviously there will be times when you must use pronouns and vague nouns like those just mentioned, but be aware of what you are doing.

Images make writing more interesting and more stimulating. Here are two short prose pieces each containing similar themes. Decide for yourself which is the livelier.

Writing without images: Do not spend your time worrying about how much you own and trying to accumulate a vast store. The chances are that your possessions will deteriorate, or they will be stolen. Greed does not make a person pleasant. You will be much nicer if you live unselfishly, loving others and sharing the little you have with them.

Writing with images: 'Do not lay up for yourselves treasures on earth where moth and rust consume and where thieves break in and steal, but lay up for yourselves treasure in heaven, where neither moth nor rust consumes and where thieves do not break in and steal. For, where your treasure is there will your heart be also.'

Images make a striking impact on the imagination. Examiners are looking for this kind of writing. One candidate was praised for her graphic account of childhood memories of the beach. She had noticed among other things:

'a dog in the sea, splashing about and shaking water over everyone ... small children being lifted under the armpits and held over the water ... rock pools to be peered into ... shells to be hunted for ... shrimps to be caught ... bladderwrack seaweed to be punctured ... whelks to be scraped off rocks .. sand between the toes ... salt in the hair ... a pleasure-boat trip and the fear of falling between the slats of the gang-plank on disembarking ... one more sandcastle to build ... one more splash in the sea ... aching legs and burnt shoulders ... sleep on the way home ...'

This candidate completed the detail with a strong final sentence:

'We never knew about the long traffic-jams – at least, not until we were much older.'

The examiner's remarks have been adapted, and the candidate's words rearranged so that you can see the kind of accuracy of observation that adds to the general effect.

Be vividly descriptive in your writing. Avoid vague statements and obvious remarks. Communicate feeling by carefully selected detail·

VAGUE	SAY SOMETHING LIKE THIS INSTEAD
We had a quick drink.	We gulped down our cokes.
It was windy and looked like rain.	Rain threatened and a strong breeze disturbed the regimented, red geraniums in the front garden.
I was surprised and excited.	My pulse began to race and I could feel the gloom lifting as it always does when life presents us with a pleasant surprise.
I was hungry.	Punctual as usual, my stomach reminded me that it was time for lunch.
I felt hot and uncomfortable.	The cold glass of water did nothing to ease my discomfort: still the perspiration dripped down my face; my body burned; my hands left a damp mark on the empty tumbler.

| *If you want to criticize instead of saying*: I thought she looked common. | Pinpoint features that say it for you: Jane wriggled her body about to imaginary music. I could not help thinking how silly she looked – almost common – in her tight school skirt with slits designed to reveal her thighs. |

(viii) *Workmanship*: Give a good impression of yourself in every part of the examination. Show respect for the examiners as well as for the examination by never being satisfied with less than your best.

Offer your best work, your best effort and your best handwriting throughout. In return you will earn the examiners' respect and win your just reward.

Lest you should think that the examiners do nothing but criticize, read what they say about outstanding workmanship:

> The best work is a delight to read. It often seems to us that the great division is not between C, B and A, but between all these and those happy few who can write with real distinction. We wish we could let them know that their work has not passed unnoticed; that we could give an 'A with distinction' to the one or two in a thousand who deserve it.

HOW TO TACKLE FREE RESPONSE COMPOSITION QUESTIONS

The Composition section is the most important part of the English Language Examination and it takes the lion's share of the marks. Some boards set one composition; others set two. All the boards set a composition that allows a free response and a wide choice; some require a controlled response as well. Most boards allow one hour for the main composition but do check your particular board's syllabus so that you know exactly what to expect.

Here is how to set about the examination:

1. *Concentrate.*
2. *Obey instructions.*
3. *Make your choice.*
4. *Plan your work.*
5. *Write your composition.* Keep an eye on the time:
   (i) 2 minutes to check instructions.
   (ii) 3 minutes to choose.
   (iii) 10 minutes to plan.
   (iv) 40 minutes to write (except AEB Syllabus II: 35 minutes).
   (v) 5 minutes to read through at the end.

Your perseverance, training and dedication are about to be put to the test. If you have followed the advice, sharpened your skills and done all that you can to develop your style, you are now ready to write continuous prose that will give you immense satisfaction.

Example 1

1 hour and 30 minutes allowed

Answer **both** *questions.*

The use of dictionaries in this examination is prohibited.

1. Choose **one** of the following for composition. About **one hour** should be spent on this question. (35 marks)

   (a) "From smoke and drums to radio and television—all means of communication are exciting." Write about the excitement and difficulties of communicating over long distances.

   (b) Describe the experiences of a famous person who sacrificed much to make the world a better place for others.

   (c) "Cats, no less liquid than their shadows,
       Offer no angles to the wind."
       What are your experiences of and thoughts about cats?

   (d) The beauty and usefulness of wood.

(e) Describe a busy scene at a railway station **or** at an airport.

(f) Trouble with my hair.

(g) "Always tell the truth, but never rat on your friends." Write a story about a person who is torn by conflicting loyalties.

(Associated Examining Board, June 1980: 025/1)

We can only work through the method together; there is no one, right answer as each is unique. At the end there is a comment about each title.

1. *Concentrate.*
2. *Obey instructions*: Answer both questions. (Question 2 is on p. 167.) Choose *one* of the following for composition. About 1 hour should be spent on this question. Notice the 35 marks.
3. *Make your choice*: If you can write from personal experience, you will have a better chance of writing an outstanding composition. Choose a title that appeals to you because you have something relevant and interesting to say. Ignore the story unless you have a flair for telling a story.
4. *Plan*:
   (i) Spend about five minutes jotting down ideas in the order they come to you while you direct your thinking on the title. Using numbers to match the different paragraphs, group your ideas together. Cross out any that you will not use so that they do not distract you.
   (ii) Think about a beginning and an ending. Can you link the two? That sometimes rounds off a composition in a satisfying way. Or do you know a relevant quotation or an interesting anecdote?
   (iii) Always remember that your first job is to catch your examiner's eye. Your first thought is unlikely to do that.
   (iv) Time spent on planning is time profitably spent. It prevents a wrong choice and eliminates the risk of repetition and padding.
   (v) Set down your ideas in a logical sequence planning paragraph by paragraph.

(vi) Check the title again. Is it singular or plural? Are there any *significant* words? Have you given balanced treatment when the title demands it? What kind of composition will you write? Will you be describing, reflecting, narrating, persuading or arguing? Often you will be doing more than one of these things during the writing of your composition.

Sometimes you may choose a discussion essay which needs a particular shape. In the space of an hour, you must present a good case being counsel for the prosecution as well as counsel for the defence, stating the case for and against with clear logic, and summing up with all the wisdom of a judge.

Once your preparation is complete, allow the plan to direct you, but do not let it restrict you. Ideas will flow as you are writing and should be included when relevant.

5. *Write*: For the next forty minutes enjoy yourself. Let the prose flow as you have practised:
  (i) Write sentences that sparkle with originality – they will if you delight in what you are doing.
 (ii) Write paragraphs alive with keenly observed detail and imagery, where appropriate, appealing to the senses – they will be if you are sincere.
 (iii) Show the examiners that you know how to punctuate, how to use words effectively, how to join ideas together, how to be mechanically accurate, but do not show off by using long words that are unnatural to your vocabulary.
 (vi) Above all, show them that you have something to say that is worth saying and that you are capable of saying it efficiently.

6. *Read through*: During the last 5 minutes read through your work with close attention. Correct any errors as neatly as you can.

Have you written the question number in the margin? Rule a line through your rough work and rule off.

Now we shall go through your choices, one by one:
(a) If you chose this one, you should have highlighted the 'excitement' and the 'difficulties' with equal emphasis. Many candidates failed to do that and produced unbalanced compositions.
(b) This was a choice for the well-informed. Unless you have adequate

knowledge about a famous person, you would be unwise to attempt it.

(c) You may have been put off by the quotation, but you should have read on. This would have been a sensible choice because the subject invites you to respond with personal experience and to explore your thoughts and feelings. Candidates who chose this one in the O-level examination produced some lively work, and the marks were significantly higher for (c) than for the other choices. Take note of that and choose the topic that allows you to write *from your own experience*. Every year the examiners stress that the best compositions are written by those who use their own experience, and the worst by those who try to imagine situations beyond their range of knowledge.

(d) If you chose this one, did you direct your thinking on to 'beauty' *and* 'usefulness'? This is like (a) in that it requires balanced treatment. In a wide-ranging subject like this, start with something that appeals to you like a beautifully carved box, or a special piece of furniture. If you keep the writing within your experience, an original composition will be born.

(e) If you were tempted by this one, I hope you found a fresh angle? It is the kind of title that attracts thousands because it is within almost everyone's experience. The majority will write a string of commonplace impressions, stating the obvious and boring the examiner. One way to try to capture the essence is to imagine that you have a television camera. Survey the scene; pick out particular people or objects that appeal to you. As the camera would move in, so your writing should spotlight the points you want to make. Fade out leaving the reader with something to ponder. Most candidates who tackled this had miserable recall and were unable to write accurately. They gave all businessmen briefcases, made all passengers stampede and panic, and most babies howl.

(f) 'Trouble' is the operative word. The title offers a chance for some lively and humorous work. Careful planning is essential otherwise ideas will not be properly developed.

(g) Unless you have a gift for story-writing, you would be wise to avoid this type of question in the examination. There are so many potential dangers, especially in credible plotting and in the punctuation of dialogue. A special skill is called for, but if you believe you can do it and the story appeals to your creative nature, read as many as you can. Analyse every short story to discover its shape and notice through whose eyes it is told. Some stories are written in the first person; others in the third person.

Warning: Another kind of question to avoid is the one that invites you to 'write a short play' unless you have practised this art during your English course.

Some boards include a picture stimulus. If yours does, use it only if it moves you to an original idea. Be careful; there must be a clear connection between your writing and the subject of the picture or the central theme illustrated by the picture. Whatever you do, do not describe the picture.

Assess Your Work

1. Is the first sentence original?
2. Have you connected your sentences with all the following: joining words from the list on p. 13; '-ing' words; and one or two of these: who, whom, whose, which, that?
3. Have you written at least five paragraphs, and preferably six?
4. Is each one indented?
5. Have the first and last paragraphs at least three sentences apiece?
6. Are the middle three or four paragraphs well-developed, having four to six sentences?
7. Are your paragraphs linked?
8. Have you written about 600 words? (If you are preparing for AEB Syllabus II you should write slightly less.) Practise until you write this number automatically. There is no need to count if you know how many words you write to a page. Examiners are experienced people who know and recognize an adequate length; they prefer quality to quantity, but do not drop below the number stated by your board. If no number is given, 600 words in an hour is about right (DO NOT EXCEED 600).
9. Have you used colons and semicolons as well as other punctuation? Are your commas *correctly* used?
10. Do your nouns and verbs project clear images?
11. Have you included substantial subject matter which is interesting

and relevant? Are your ideas illustrated from your personal experience or what you have read?

12. Is your line of thought/argument/narrative/description intelligible? (It will be if your work is arranged in an orderly manner and your language appropriate.)

13. Is your spelling accurate?

14. Does your workmanship shine?

Taking all the above into account, which one of these words would you use to classify your composition: excellent, capable, satisfactory, weak, unsatisfactory? Or, if you prefer, would you grade it A, B, C, D or E?

Excellent (A): A composition in this class is alive with original ideas that are properly developed and illustrated. The quality of the writing is first-class and the reader is involved and interested.

Capable (B): The subject matter is adequate and the ideas quite well developed. The work is technically accurate and written in an appropriate style that includes some personal experience.

Satisfactory (C): The ideas are less interesting but relevant. The writing is lifeless but correct on the whole.

Weak (D): The ideas are undeveloped; the work is without structure. It contains careless and colloquial English and the general effect is scrappy with some repetition of ideas.

Unsatisfactory (E): Work in this class fails to communicate adequately.

Please note that different boards mark in different ways and the grades and marks listed above are not common to every examination board. Nothing in the way of marks here is official, but I have worked out a rough guide for you to judge your work by, based on information from various examiners' reports and their criteria.

Example 2

SECTION B

6. "Amazing, unrepeatable bargain!" Complete this entry in the "small-ads" section of a newspaper, and then relate what happened when the advertisement was answered.

7. Waiting rooms.

8. Describe a place that a casual visitor might consider unattractive, but that you have become fond of over a period of time.

· 9. Thoughts on the prospect of leaving school or college

10. "To step over the low wall that divides
Road from concrete walk above the shore
Brings back sharply something known long before—
The miniature gaiety of seasides.
Everything crowds under the low horizon:
Steep beach, blue water, towels, red bathing caps,
The small hushed waves' repeated fresh collapse
Up the warm yellow sand, and further off
A white steamer stuck in the afternoon—
Still going on, all of it, still going on!"

(PHILIP LARKIN)

What memories do you have of childhood visits to the beach?

(Associated Examining Board, June 1980: 069/1)

25 marks are given for each section so spend 50 minutes on each composition (Section A is on p. 159). Choose one topic from Section B.

6 This gives an opportunity to write a narrative, but if you have not mastered the skill of punctuating direct speech you must resist the temptation, however much you feel you would be lively and interesting. If you do attempt one like this, avoid an ending that can be guessed in advance, or one that leaves the reader in the air.

7. The best candidates would make comments about a variety of waiting rooms illustrated from personal experience and reading. They would compare and contrast these, and, with a keen eye for detail, would write clearly described accounts. Their thoughts and feelings would be ably expressed. The worst would misread the title and produce a weary, predictable list of irrelevant facts about a visit to a dentist.

8. Notice the wording. The significant word is 'unattractive' What

must you do then? Choose a place that is recognizably unattractive like a slag-heap or a multi-storey car park. Somehow you must grow to like this place. Ask how? why? when?

9. In this kind of question, remember the other 499 scripts your examiner may be marking and be original. Write about your thoughts, feelings and experiences. The best work would highlight memorable moments of life at school and consider your development from child to young adult. Your personal opinion of your future life would also be relevant and interesting.

10. The stimulus, Philip Larkin's poem, provides a clear clue. Fresh images are needed for a lively composition. Do not bore your examiner with a humdrum account. See the beach in your mind's eye and be involved through all your senses. You will then produce a first-class account. There is an additional note about this composition on pp. 140–41.

Example 3

1. **COMPOSITION** (50 marks).
   Choose a subject from the list below about which you can write interestingly; plan your composition according to the nature of the material and the form (narrative, descriptive, discursive, dramatic, etc.); write in an appropriate style and take care with grammar, spelling, and punctuation. Your composition should be 450 words or more in length, but, apart from that, will be assessed on the quality, not the quantity, of what you have written.

   (*a*) A leap in the dark.

   (*b*) Write to your future grandchildren, giving an impression of your present way of life, thoughts, and feelings as a young person. Consider what they might find interesting to learn about in fifty years' time.

   (*c*) Changing fashions.
   (You may care to discuss why and how fashions in clothes, manners, or attitudes change.)

   (*d*) The happiest (or the saddest) event in your life so far.

(*e*)   'The most important thing in the Olympic Games
       is not to win but to take part, just as the most
       important thing in life is not the triumph but the
       struggle. The essential thing is not to have con-
       quered but to have fought well.' (*Pierre de
       Coubertin, founder of the modern Olympic Games.*)
How far do you consider this ideal still to be the most important
thing about the Games?

(*f*) Someone you hope never to meet again.
(You may need to describe the person's appearance, views, and
behaviour in detail in order to account for your reaction.)

(*g*) Write a short play by continuing the dialogue below in a manner
which develops the dramatic situation.
(Do not copy out the extract before you begin your work, but
you are advised to continue its method of setting out the
dialogue. If you wish, you may introduce one or two more
characters or add a further scene.)

*As the curtain rises, Sally Brooks and her father, Derek Brooks, are
sitting in the front row of desks in a school classroom. Derek is in
his late forties and Sally is sixteen years old; both are sitting
tense and motionless.*

*Derek gets up quickly and awkwardly as Helen Davis, an attrac-
tive young teacher of about twenty-five, comes into the room.*

Helen: Oh, is this your father, Sally?
Sally: Yes, Miss Davis.
Helen: How are you, Mr Brooks? Please sit down. I'm Sally's
        class teacher.
        (*She and Mr Brooks shake hands and sit down.*)
        It was kind of you to come straight away. I'll tell you
        why I had to write to you as I did.

Derek: My wife and I are both quite worried.

(*h*) Write a story, a description, or an essay suggested by one of the
pictures on the accompanying sheet.

(Your composition may be directly about the subject of the picture, or may take only some suggestions from it, but *there must
be some clear connection between the picture and your composition.*)

(University of London, June 1980: 160/1)

Rubric: 'Choose a subject from the list below about which you can write *interestingly*; *plan* your composition according to the nature of the material and the form (narrative, descriptive, discursive, dramatic, etc.). Write in an *appropriate style* and *take care* with grammar, spelling, and punctuation. Your composition should be 450 words or more in length, but, apart from that, will be assessed on the *quality*, not the quantity, of what you have written.'

Make sure you read and note the rubric. It may change; you must always check it. Words are not underlined on the examination paper; here, I have drawn your attention to particular words, but all are important.

(a) This was not a popular choice probably because candidates did not understand the meaning. If you take a leap in the dark, you take some action without foreseeing the consequences. How many times have you done that in your life? If one experience stands out, you have the material for an original composition.

(b) Note that there are two important parts to this question. You are asked to write to your grandchildren so a letter would be the appropriate form. The style should be informal but not careless.

(c) The little word 'or' was disregarded by many candidates. If you are invited to discuss 'something', 'something' *or* 'something else', you must not discuss all three. The word 'and' would have been used instead of 'or' if all three were to have been discussed.

(d) Some moving compositions were written in response to this title and one could only hope that time would heal the open wounds of those who chose the saddest event. Again there was misreading and some wrote about more than one event.

(e) When you misunderstand or misread a title, your work becomes irrelevant. Choose a topic that you are certain about for maximum efficiency. Those who followed the Games and understood the implications of this question were able to produce skilful work sensibly illustrated.

(f) With so much help in this question it would be difficult to be irrelevant. Candidates responded with enthusiasm, using personal experience and keen observation like this one:

As soon as I saw the old lady I felt an icy shiver down my spine. Her face was brown and gnarled with age like the bark of an ancient tree. Amid the many wrinkles and folds of shrivelled skin a hooked nose protruded. There was a wart on the end of it. Her two black, beady eyes darted eagerly from side to side under her black, felt hat; stringy wisps of hair hung across her face, and her mouth was lost in the wrinkles. An enormous, black cloak shrouded her body. I had seen her double in the wicked witch of a childhood fairy-tale.

(g) and (h): see p. 147.

Example 4

1. COMPOSITION (40 marks).

Choose a subject from the list below about which you can write inter-estingly and relevantly; plan your composition according to the nature of the material and the form (narrative, descriptive, dis-cursive, dramatic, etc.); write in an appropriate style and take care with grammar, spelling, and punctuation. Your composition should be 450 words or more in length, but, apart from that, will be assessed on the quality, not the quantity, of what you have written.

(*a*) The uphill struggle.

(*b*) So far you have spent some 13,000 hours of your life in school. Which of these hours have been most memorable for you? (You may like to describe several experiences chosen from different stages of your time in school or prefer to comment in detail on one or two.)

(*c*) The street-market.
(You may wish to describe the people, the activities, and the stalls to be seen or to comment on the part played by a street-market in your district.)

(*d*) Telling tales.

(*e*) Animals you have known.
(Discuss and comment on their pleasant and unpleasant characteristics and show what you have learnt from observing their behaviour.)

(*f*) The fascination and challenge of modern technology.
(Describe your reactions to recent developments in

machines, computers, and other equipment and their effects on work and leisure.)

(g) *David McKenzie, a young man of eighteen, is sitting at the table of the living-room making a model from a kit; his sister, Jacky, a bright-eyed nervous teenager, is curled up in an armchair watching television. Their father, who has just returned from work, is recovering his spirits by trying to read the evening newspaper.*

There is an insistent ringing of the doorbell, Mrs McKenzie is heard going to answer it, and there are muffled sounds of a serious conversation outside. The door of the living-room opens violently. She appears, disturbed and shaking.

Mr. McKenzie (casually looking up): What is it, dear?

Mrs. McKenzie (breathlessly): There's a policeman at the door.

David: Oh, no!

Jacky quickly unrolls herself from the chair and switches off the television; she looks anxiously at her father and bursts into tears.

Either (i) Write a short play by continuing the dialogue in a manner which develops the dramatic situation. (You are advised to continue the method of setting out the dialogue, but *do not copy out the extract.* If you wish, you may introduce one or two more characters or add a further scene.)

Or (ii) Discuss the role of the policeman in the community. (You may wish to give examples of the varied work done by policemen, to comment on the attitudes of the public to them, and to estimate the contribution they make to society.)

(h) Write a story, a description, or an essay suggested by *one* of the pictures on the accompanying sheet. (Your composition should be directly about the subject of the picture or take some central suggestion(s) from it: *there must be some clear connection between the picture and your composition.*)

(University of London, January 1982: 160/1)

The changed rubric is significant. Suddenly two extra words have appeared: '*and relevantly*'. This board now gives 40 marks for the composition, as extra marks have been allocated for Summary and Directed Writing.

(a) The term 'an uphill struggle' is used to describe a very difficult task. The subject matter must be about a very difficult task. There is always the temptation to write about the first idea that comes into your head. Other people will have the same idea. Think again. A short title like this must be the central theme of your composition. It is not enough to say, right at the end, that such-and-such a thing was an uphill struggle.

(b) Pay attention to the guidelines in brackets – they are put there for *your* benefit. Consider what makes an event 'memorable'. As far as possible choose incidents that you did not have to share with the rest of your year group to avoid duplicating what other candidates will be writing. If you must include first day memories and the school trip abroad, find a fresh angle so that your work stands out among the predictable compositions. For instance, your school friend will probably be your lifelong friend. How did you meet?

(c) Attempt this one only if you have visited a street-market.

(d) This title has more than one meaning. Which would you choose?

(e) The title is plural so when you organize your material, plan with several animals in mind. The danger here would be to write at length on one or two animals and to skimp the remainder. Make sure you include everything requested in the brackets.

(f) Your writing must be enthusiastic when you discuss 'fascination' and convincing when you describe your reactions to recent developments. You need special knowledge for this one. Rough out your ideas to see how far you could develop your paragraphs. If you have not thought much about the new technology before, this composition would be a difficult assignment to complete in an hour.

(g) (i) If you have mastered the skill of writing in dramatic form, consider this one. Otherwise go on to (ii) – or another question.

(ii) You should have sufficient knowledge to discuss this question. Use your personal observation, anything you have learned from the media, and even facts you can remember from the passages for close reading in this book. Beware of writing at length on 'the varied work done by policemen' and forgetting 'to comment on the attitudes of the public to them' and 'to estimate the contribution they make to society'.

(h) The picture stimulus is not the 'unimaginative's guide to instant composition', as some seem to think. Nor is it a springboard for a hackneyed spy or crime story; nor a starting-point that offers an opportunity to re-tell a film or a play that you have seen. Such plans fail miserably because secondhand material cannot be lively, convincing or original. More often than not it is irrelevant, too.

The picture stimulus – and lines of poetry sometimes used in the same way – is intended to evoke an original response. Your composition should be directly about the subject of the picture, or take some central suggestion from it.

Example 5

Note that this is Part I of a paper. *Read the rubric.* There are two exercises. You are advised to write first on your chosen subject in Part I, and then to answer Part II (see p. 161).

Remember to pay attention all through the paper to spelling, punctuation and the construction of sentences.

PART I

Write a composition on **one** of the following subjects. You should cover about two sides of the writing paper and **not more than three.**

[70]

Either, (*a*) Pocket-money.

Or, (*b*) If cinemas were all closed down permanently, would you feel seriously deprived?

Or, (*c*)   'God gave all men all earth to love
          But since our hearts are small,
        Ordained, for each, one spot should prove
          Beloved over all ...'   (RUDYARD KIPLING)

Describe the 'one spot' which means most to you.

Or, (*d*) Describe an act of kindness which you have witnessed or have read about.

Or, (*e*) 'A dented halo': write about the events, which, temporarily at least, spoiled somebody's good reputation.

(Oxford Local Examinations, November 1980: 1801/1)

(a) If you have some definite views about this and plenty of illustrative material, you could write an interesting composition. Be positive and develop a clear line of thought at the planning stage.

(b) You must have knowledge, experience and strong feelings if you attempt a topic like this one.

(c) The main requirement for this question is sincerity. Indeed, such a quality is necessary for all kinds of writing, but unless you mean what you say in describing a place that means most to you, you will not convince your readers.

(d) If something springs to mind, develop it. You are more likely to succeed with an act of kindness you have seen than one you have read about. There is a danger in inventing one without direct experience to back it, because the involvement and emotions will not ring true.

(e) This is an unusual title allowing an interesting response. Fiction writers could probably produce an amusing, yet credible, story; the rest could write a composition from a store of personal experience.

Example 6

PART I

Write a composition on **one** of the following subjects. You should cover about two sides of the writing paper and **not more than three.**

[70]

Either, (*a*) If you were in charge of television broadcasting, what alterations would you make, and why?

Or, (*b*) An interview remembered. (The expectations, journey, tension, actual interview, and your feelings afterwards may all be considered.)

Or, (*c*) The river.

Or, (*d*) Speed.

Or, (*e*) 'Last Saturday, at the house near the end of the road....'

(Oxford Local Examinations, June 1981: 1801/1)

Again, this is Part I of a paper. (For Part II see p. 168.)

(a) Unless you have a flair for writing and some positive ideas about television, avoid this one. You need to be an experienced, well-informed viewer to attempt such a composition, but, if you feel capable, go ahead. Remember to put titles of programmes in inverted commas and to use capital letters for the main words.

(b) For a candidate who has attended an interview, this title offers an opportunity for an interesting and relevant composition. Follow the guidelines in brackets, remembering that the interview is the focal point of your work.

(c) and (d) One word titles are vague, and unprepared candidates often fall into the trap of writing in a disorganized way. When you are faced with choices like these, remember the television camera. Move your mental eye about in a similar manner, focusing first on one and then on another aspect of the single word title. In 600 words there is time for only one particular viewpoint. Keep that one thread running through the detail you build up and you will create a final effect that is satisfying.

(e) If you have experience of a happening of some kind at a neighbour's house you can write convincingly. Do not attempt to make this a story unless you are a story-teller. If you have developed this skill you will know how important it is either to create credible characters and to invent conflict tests for them before the problem is resolved in an unpredictable way; or to invent a story that makes a profound comment on life through the behaviour of the characters.

HOW TO TACKLE CONTROLLED RESPONSE COMPOSITION QUESTIONS

The syllabus states: 'These (compositions) in Section A will be factual or controversial with the subjects clearly delimited, and will call for a controlled response' ('delimited' means 'within marked limits' or 'within certain boundaries').

Section A of this paper requires a 50-minute composition with a *controlled response*. (Section B of this paper is printed on p. 148.)

Example 7

1 hour and 45 minutes allowed

Choose two subjects for composition, one from Section A and one from Section B. 25 marks are given for each section. Consequently, you should spend about the same time on each composition.

Greater credit will be given for expression and for arrangement of ideas than for mere length, but an adequate treatment will be expected.

The use of dictionaries in this examination is prohibited.

SECTION A

1. How important to you is it to have a room that you can call your own? Explain your point of view.

2. Give a brief description of a radio or a television series that has appealed to you, and explain why you enjoyed it.

3. The pleasures and pains of acquiring a skill, such as learning to play a musical instrument, or becoming proficient in a sport or a hobby.

4. If you had complete freedom of choice, which country would you prefer to live in, and why? (You may choose the country you already live in.)

5. Give the arguments for and against lotteries, organized locally or nationally, in order to raise money for good causes.

(Associated Examining Board, June 1980: 069/1)

1. Candidates who did not plan repeated themselves and produced rambling, incoherent work. The title calls for a factual account of the importance you attach to having a room of your own. The limits are clearly marked and you must not stray from them while explaining your point of view.
2. Notice the word 'brief'; an outline of the series is all that is required, not a long, involved account. Convey your pleasure in your explanation of why you enjoyed the series. Remember the inverted commas for the title.

3. There was much misreading and misunderstanding of this title. For one thing, some candidates wrote about playing a game instead of *learning* to play it; for another, they wrote about several skills instead of keeping within the limits set which were 'the pleasures and pains of acquiring *a* skill'. It seems many did not understand the exact meaning of 'acquiring'. Never attempt a composition that contains a word you do not understand. It is far better to choose something else.

4. The compositions in this question were well done; almost all the candidates chose to extol the virtues of their own country in some positive writing.

5. It is important to understand the limits of this title, and others like it. It is no good listing a number of lotteries of different kinds; it is even worse to write about other ways of raising money for charity, because such ideas are beyond the bounds of the question. This is a controversial subject and requires clear discussion putting points for and against raffles, and other kinds of games of chance, in order to raise money for good causes.

In section A, you must do one of two things. You must either write a straightforward factual account of something, or write discursively – that is, discuss something that is debatable.

Keep within the confines of the question and choose one that you completely understand. It is not wise to guess the meaning of a word in such an important part of the English Language Examination.

PRACTICAL WRITING

Practical writing is brief and to the point. It is the language of facts, instructions, reports, formal letters, explanations, accounts and statements. As it is widely used in every kind of business and profession, it must be exact in every detail.

Little did you realize when you explained a process or the rules of a game to a younger person, or the homework to a friend, or described your room to a relation, or gave directions to a stranger that you were practising a skill you would need for O-level. It was not difficult, was it? You may be asked to do any of those things or something else equally straightforward.

The procedure does not vary:

1. Concentrate.
2. Think out your content.
3. Arrange it in a coherent order.
4. Stick to the point.
5. Write in correct English and always in continuous prose All forms of practical writing must be arranged in paragraphs.

Letters

The most useful skill for you to acquire is probably the art of letter-writing. Do not jump to the wrong conclusion that the other forms of practical writing are less important. For examination purposes they are on a par.

Your letter of application for your first job will be the most important you ever have to write. Your success can stand or fall on the impression that you make. Time and time again successful pupils have said that they were congratulated on their letters. Believe me, efficient letters do matter.

Make sure you can write a correct letter of application, and other formal letters will present no problems. The basic shape is the same. Here are some points of reference for you so that you know what to do; we can do no better than to start on an O-level paper. This question is Part II of the paper printed on p. 156. It provides some very useful guidelines.

Example 8

PART II

You should understand that this question is designed to test your accuracy in the writing of English and in your use of the material provided. You are advised not to cover more than about **one** side of the writing paper. [30]

Messrs. Stanton, Blackwood and Rob, Stangate Street, Witton, Barsetshire, have advertised various vacancies, in one of which you are interested. Write a letter (set out in full) to Mr. Arthur Thompson, the Personnel Manager, applying for this job. State the particular vacancy for which you are applying. Give your age and qualifications, indicating subjects and grades in Certificate examinations. (You may assume some appropriate successes.) Mention your school record, your particular interests, and the name and address of a person who is not related to you and to whom reference may be made. State when you will be available for interview, and say why you think you may be a suitable member of the firm.

N.B. You are free to choose the nature of the firm's business activities.

(Oxford Local Examinations, November 1980:1801/1)

11, Harebell Lane,
Witton,
Barsetshire. WN2 6XY
25 May 1984

Mr. A. Thompson,
Personnel Manager,
Messrs. Stanton, Blackwood and Rob,
Stangate Street,
Witton,
Barsetshire.

Dear Sir,

With reference to your advertisement in last night's 'Witton Echo', I should like to be considered for the post of Receptionist/Clerk in your publishing firm.

I am seventeen and due to leave Witton High School at the end of next month, having completed a year's general course in the Sixth Form. Before that I passed in seven G.C.E. O-level subjects with A grades in History, English Language and English Literature; B grades in Biology, French and Geography; and a C grade in Mathematics.

During the last two years I have been involved in a wide range of school activities including drama, community service and tennis. I have been a School Prefect and taken considerable responsibility as School Librarian. In this role I have developed a lively interest in books and learnt much about classification, issuing, ordering, costing and stocktaking. More importantly, I have discovered that I have a knack of getting on with people of all ages who use the facilities of the School Library. I enjoy helping them.

I should like to make a career in publishing in a large, well-established firm, where there would be opportunities for promotion after I had proved my worth and given reliable service. I believe I have the necessary qualities, and my school record is not without value.

My Headmaster has agreed to supply you with a reference. His name and address are as follows:

Mr. N. J. Stone, B.A.,
   Witton High School,
      Southover Avenue,
         Witton.

Mr. Stone has said that I may attend an interview at any time convenient to you.

Yours faithfully,

Jane French

Important: Sign your name legibly. It is not polite to scribble a signature. When you make your first application, it is unnecessary to print your name under the signature.

The rubric says do not cover more than about one side. As twenty lines have been used for the letter-format,* *this answer does not exceed the recommended length.*

Here are some points to note:

1. Write your address in the top right-hand corner with each line indented and punctuated. Although punctuation is gradually disappearing from addresses, several examiners still expect to see it. Each line ends with a comma until you come to the county; a full stop is required here. There is no punctuation on the postal code. The code can be written on the same line as the county at the top of your letter; on the envelope it must be last on a line by itself.

2. Write the date under the address. There are various acceptable ways, but avoid abbreviations. They do not give a good impression.

---

* addresses and the subscription

3. Leave a line.

4. Write the name of the person to whom the letter is being written followed by the address. Although the question printed the name 'Arthur', a young person applying for a post should address him as Mr. A. Thompson. Notice the full stops after Mr. A. and Messrs. Notice the capital letters as well.

5. Leave a line.

6. Begin: 'Dear Sir,'. Do not forget the capital letter and the comma (see the chart below).

7. Begin the first word of the letter under the 'S' of 'Sir'.

8. You may have some problems with capital letters in words like 'school', 'drama' and so on. Your best guide is to use a capital letter when you are referring to a particular place or thing or person, and a small letter when you are using the words in a general sense.

9 *The layout* of the letter is important. Leave a space or frame around it. Letters that are cramped or badly arranged do not give much of an impression.

10. *Paragraphing:* Paragraphs are important. In this particular letter notice:
    (i) A brief introduction in which you state your reason for writing.
    (ii) The main body of the letter arranged in three paragraphs.
    (iii) A brief conclusion.

11. *Relevance:* In the worked example the content does not stray from demands of the question. This is an exercise to test your ability to write in a conventional register, so you must keep your letter formal and brief. Use common sense, though. You must write enough, without padding, to score the marks available.

12. In any letter of application for a job, use the guidelines set out in this question which are as follows:
    (i) State the vacancy for which you are applying.
    (ii) Give your age and qualifications, indicating subjects and grades in Certificate examinations.
    (iii) Mention your school record and your particular interests.
    (iv) Mention the name and address of a person who is not related to you and to whom reference may be made.

   (v) State when you will be available for interview.

   (vi) Say why you think you may be a suitable member of the firm.

You can adapt the content of this letter to your own particular interests, qualifications and school record.

This is a table to show you how to begin and end your letters:

ADDRESSEE	BEGIN	END
A person you do not know; a firm or organization:	Dear Sir, Dear Madam,	Yours faithfully,
An editor of a newspaper:	Sir,	Yours, etc.,*
A person known to you by name, but on a formal basis like teachers or employers:	Dear Mr. —, Dear Mrs. —, Dear Miss —,	Yours sincerely,
Friends and relations:	Dear —, My dear —, (or any way you like)	With love, Yours, As ever, (or anything else you choose)

*This may seem strange to you but it is considered correct for letters to the press. Notice the punctuation.

But instead of writing practice letters in this part of the syllabus, why not write real letters? You will enjoy receiving answers and, who knows? you may have one published.

Set each letter out like the one in the worked example, except letters to family and friends, and then proceed as follows:

1. State your reason for writing.
2.   (i) *Ask your question* (do this as clearly as you can); or
   (ii) *Make your complaint* (politely); or
  (iii) *State your case*: assemble all the facts and write briefly. Politely persuade your reader that consideration should be given to the points you have made; or

(iv) *Air your view or grievance*: While respecting the right of others to hold opposing views, be confident in expressing yours. Nothing will be gained by rudeness or spoiling for a verbal battle. Do not let your indignation lead you into verbal violence. Remain detached and formal.

Sign your name clearly, and print 'MISS' *in brackets* if appropriate. Your signature consists of your Christian name and surname.

If you expect a reply to any of your letters, enclose a stamped and addressed envelope.

Reports

These include articles and accounts and are similar to summaries in tone. If you have to write a report of a meeting, discussion, performance or anything at all, your job is to write continuous prose that shows clear thought and orderly presentation. Plan your points first, arrange your material in paragraphs and write with a particular audience in mind – in addition to the examiner, of course.

(i)   State the nature of the report.

(ii) Describe where the event took place.

(iii) Mention the purpose of the activity.

(iv) Report on the suggestions made, and those involved in the activity.

(v)   Mention the conclusions that can be drawn.

Statement

This is similar to a report, the only difference being that it is a statement of your opinion and therefore is written in the first person. Be brief, as before, but include enough substance to earn a comfortable number of the available marks.

In a half-hour question, one side of examination paper written in average sized handwriting (about eight words per line) is the accepted length.

Description of an Everyday Action

Without being too long-winded describe the tools or ingredients that will be required. Follow that by explaining how to perform the operation and the reason for doing it. Avoid the recipe or note-making approach. Explain everything that relates to the process in continuous prose. Again cover one side of examination paper.

Example 9

2. Answer **one** of the following. About **half an hour** should be spent on this question. (15 marks)
 (a) Describe the ideal layout and the essential equipment of **one** of the following:
  (i) a kitchen for a household of four;
  (ii) a workshop-shed;
  (iii) a study-bedroom for a student.
 (b) Write a letter to the editor of your local newspaper, telling of an unidentified flying object (U.F.O.) you and a friend saw. Then write a second letter from a reader who is doubtful about your sighting.
 (c) What advice would you offer to an overseas pupil or student who is new to your school or college to help him or her to settle down as quickly as possible?
 (d) During a lesson at school or college you are invited to speak briefly for or against **one** of the following:
  (i) that there should be four terms in the school or college year;
  (ii) that there should be an increase in the number of football teams including both men and women;
  (iii) that a licence to drive a car should be obtainable at the age of 16.
 Write your speech.

(Associated Examining Board, June 1980: 025/1)

2. (a) (i), (ii) and (iii) You should be able to describe the layout and essential equipment in three well-structured paragraphs. Remember the necessity for orderly arrangement of relevant subject-matter stated in the syllabus.
 (b) You would have a chance to show your letter-writing skill in a question like this. Keep faithfully to the point and be exact in the letter-format.

  (c) The important aspects to emphasize are those that will help the student to settle down. Put yourself in his place so that you will realize his apprehension and be able to give advice to lessen this.

  (d) There are certain conventions for speech-making. If you have had experience of public speaking either as a participant or member of the audience, you could try this one. Otherwise leave it alone.

Example 10

PART II

You should understand that this question is designed to test your accuracy in the writing of English and in your use of the material provided. You are advised not to cover more than about **one side of** the writing paper.   **[30]**

Write an article for your school magazine about Colonel Munro, your new Chairman of Governors, selecting your information from the paragraph below:

MUNRO, Henry Antony, b. Ascot, 1932. 2nd son of Antony Paul Munro and Emily Ann (née Topping). Educated at Ascot School. Captain of the School, Captain of Cricket, Higher Certificate with distinctions in Mathematics, Physics and Geography. Subsidiary subjects Russian and French. National Service in Royal Army Service Corps 1951. Commissioned 2nd Lieutenant in Royal Blankshire Regt. Oct. 1952. Regular commissions Lieut. 1954, Captain 1960, seconded as a Temporary Major (Instructor) in Royal Thailand Army 1962. Special duties in Burma, India, and Thailand. Lt. Colonel 1970. Wounded in Ireland 1978. Awarded D.S.O. and invalided out of army. Publications: *Indian Butterflies, Thai Temples, The Irish House* (novel). Married Mary Smith 1971, sons born 1973 and 1975. Home: London.

(Oxford Local Examinations, June 1981: 1801/1)

This worked example is Part II of the paper discussed in Example 6 on p. 157. It is only a suggested answer. You try it as well and see if you can make a better job of it.

It is my pleasure to record that Colonel H. A. Munro, D.S.O., is to be our new Chairman of Governors. His qualifications are awe-inspiring and each one of us will benefit as a result of his wide experience and diverse talents.

At Ascot School where he was educated, he made a name for himself in several fields. A born leader, he became Captain of the School and Captain of Cricket; a born scholar, he reached academic heights in the Higher Certificate results, being awarded a distinction in each of his three specialist subjects: Mathematics, Physics and Geography. Not only that, but he is a linguist, too, and speaks Russian and French which he studied as subsidiary subjects.

After his brilliant school career, he enlisted in the Royal Army Service Corps for compulsory National Service in 1951 and later decided to make the Army his life. He was commissioned in the regular Army in 1952 with the rank of 2nd Lieutenant, and by 1960 he had been promoted to Captain. In 1962 he took the opportunity of being seconded to Burma, India and Thailand with the rank of Temporary Major (Instructor) in the Royal Thailand Army and by 1970 he had risen to the rank of Lt. Colonel.

During his overseas service, Colonel Munro became interested in Indian butterflies and Thai temples. He has had books published on these subjects, and also written a novel entitled 'The Irish House'.

Colonel Munro was on duty in Northern Ireland when his notable service career was brought to an untimely end. He was wounded in 1978, invalided out of the Army and decorated for his bravery. We are privileged to have so illustrious a gentleman as our Chairman, and proud to welcome him to our School.

School magazines vary in style, presentation and register, but you should be guided by the rubric which reminds you that the 'question is designed to test your accuracy in the writing of English'. A colloquial style would, therefore, be inappropriate. We had to *select* from the information. There was no directive to include it all. As you can see, I have left out his family particulars as I considered that these were the least important for inclusion in a school magazine and, as it is important to keep as near as possible to the required length, I had to leave something out.

A FINAL WORD

Speaking and writing are natural skills and, like all talents, they improve with regular practice.

Through language we explore experience; emotion; the essence of existence. Until all that we feel and think finds its natural outlet in coherent, fluent, and accurate words, we have not come of age.

'Reading maketh a full man; conference a ready man; and writing an exact man.'

FRANCIS BACON (1561–1626), 'Of Studies'

MORE ABOUT PENGUINS, PELICANS AND PUFFINS

For further information about books available from Penguins please write to Dept EP, Penguin Books Ltd, Harmondsworth, Middlesex UB7 0DA.

In the U.S.A.: For a complete list of books available from Penguins in the United States write to Dept DG, Penguin Books, 299 Murray Hill Parkway, East Rutherford, New Jersey 07073.

In Canada: For a complete list of books available from Penguins in Canada write to Penguin Books Canada Ltd, 2801 John Street, Markham, Ontario L3R 1B4.

In Australia: For a complete list of books available from Penguins in Australia write to the Marketing Department, Penguin Books Australia Ltd, P.O. Box 257, Ringwood, Victoria 3134.

In New Zealand: For a complete list of books available from Penguins in New Zealand write to the Marketing Department, Penguin Books (N.Z.) Ltd, Private Bag, Takapuna, Auckland 9.

In India: For a complete list of books available from Penguins in India write to Penguin Overseas Ltd, 706 Eros Apartments, 56 Nehru Place, New Delhi 110019.

PENGUIN PASSNOTES

Carefully tailored to the requirements of the main examination boards (for O-level or CSE exams), Penguin Passnotes are an invaluable companion to your studies.

Covering a wide range of English Literature texts, as well as many other subjects, Penguin Passnotes will include:

ENGLISH LITERATURE

As You Like It
Henry IV, Part I
Julius Caesar
Macbeth
The Merchant of Venice
Romeo and Juliet
Twelfth Night
The Prologue to the Canterbury Tales
Cider With Rosie

Great Expectations
Jane Eyre
A Man For All Seasons
The Mayor of Casterbridge
Pride and Prejudice
Silas Marner
To Kill a Mockingbird
The Woman in White
Wuthering Heights

and OTHER AREAS

Biology
Chemistry
Economics
English Language
French
Geography

Human Biology
Mathematics
Modern Mathematics
Modern World History
Physics